DATE DUE

~~MAY 08 1992~~	
~~OCT ...~~	
SEP 30 1992	
DEC 17 1993	
~~MAR 22 1999~~	
~~APR 14 1999~~	
MAY 24 1999	
DEC 13 2002	

Cat. No. 23-221

STEPHEN CRANE

Modern Critical Views

Continued at back of book

Modern Critical Views

STEPHEN CRANE

Edited and with an introduction by
Harold Bloom
Sterling Professor of the Humanities
Yale University

CHELSEA HOUSE PUBLISHERS ◊ 1987
New York ◊ NewHaven ◊ Philadelphia

© 1987 by Chelsea House Publishers, a division of Chelsea
House Educational Communications, Inc.
95 Madison Avenue, New York, NY 10016
345 Whitney Avenue, New Haven, CT 06511
5068B West Chester Pike, Edgemont, PA 19028

Introduction © 1987 by Harold Bloom

Printed and bound in the United States of America

10 9 8 7 6 5 4 3 2

∞ The paper used in this publication meets the minimum
requirements of the American National Standard for Permanence
of Paper for Printed Library Materials, Z39.48–1984.

Library of Congress Cataloging-in-Publication Data
Stephen Crane.
(Modern critical views)
Bibliography: p.
Includes index.
1. Crane, Stephen, 1871–1900—Criticism and
interpretation. I. Bloom, Harold. II. Series.
PS1449.C85Z925 1987   813'.4   86–18857
ISBN 0–87754–694–0 (alk. paper)

Contents

Editor's Note

This book brings together a representative selection of the best criticism available upon the writings of Stephen Crane. The essays are arranged here in the chronological order of their original publication. I am grateful to Frank Menchaca for his erudition and judgment in helping to edit this volume.

My introduction concerns itself with the extraordinary originality of *The Red Badge of Courage,* particularly in its representation of battle. The chronological sequence of criticism begins with the poet John Berryman's psychological overview of Stephen Crane, and continues with the informed meditation upon the relation between Crane's personality and his poetry by another accomplished poet, Daniel G. Hoffman.

Stanley Wertheim traces Crane's vision to the Methodist religious context of his childhood. This is followed by three studies of short stories. Daniel Weiss, in his psychoanalytical reading of Crane's story "The Blue Hotel," sees it as an intensive and masterful study of fear, while Marston LaFrance analyzes Crane's remarkable short story "The Open Boat." In a reading of Crane's "city sketches," Alan Trachtenberg shrewdly sketches the socioeconomic context of Crane's maturing years.

The important critical issue of Crane's literary impressionism in the *Red Badge* is surveyed by James Nagel, who views the novel as a study in perception, distortion, and subsequent realization. Harold Kaplan, emphasizing another aesthetic strand in Crane, judges him rather as a naturalist, working through the implications of a vitalistic stance.

From the perspective of feminist literary criticism, Carol Hurd Green finds in Crane's preoccupation with "fallen women" an immature obsession with what he judged to be "women's incapacity for loyalty," particularly as exemplified in *Maggie* and "The Monster."

We return to *The Red Badge of Courage* with Chester L. Wolford's study of Crane's powerful control of epic consciousness. This book concludes with a section of Michael Fried's brilliant exploration of the analogues between the painter Eakins and the *Red Badge*. Fried finds an equation of artistic representation with processes of disfiguration, thus giving us a fresh perspective that may be prophetic of the future criticism of Crane's greatest achievement.

Introduction

I

Stephen Crane's contribution to the canon of American literature is fairly slight in bulk: one classic short novel, three vivid stories, and two or three ironic lyrics. *The Red Badge of Courage*; "The Open Boat," "The Blue Hotel," and "The Bride Comes to Yellow Sky"; "War Is Kind" and "A man adrift on a slim spar" —a single small volume can hold them all. Crane was dead at twenty-eight, after a frantic life, but a longer existence probably would not have enhanced his achievement. He was an exemplary American writer, flaring in the forehead of the morning sky and vanishing in the high noon of our evening land. An original, if not quite a Great Original, he prophesied Hemingway and our other journalist-novelists and still seems a forerunner of much to come.

The Red Badge of Courage is Crane's undoubted masterwork. Each time I reread it, I am surprised afresh, particularly by the book's originality, which requires a reader's act of recovery, because Crane's novel has been so influential. To write about battle in English, since Crane, is to be shadowed by Crane. Yet Crane, who later saw warfare in Cuba and between the Greeks and the Turks in his work as a correspondent, had experienced no fighting when he wrote *The Red Badge of Courage*. There is no actual experience that informs Crane's version of the Battle of Chancellorsville, one of the most terrible carnages of the American Civil War. Yet anyone who has gone through warfare, from the time of the novel's publication (1895) until now, has testified to Crane's uncanny accuracy at the representation of battle. *The Red Badge of Courage* is an impressionist's triumph, in the particular sense that "impressionist" had in the literature of the nineties, a Paterian sense that went back to the emphasis upon *seeing* in Carlyle, Emerson, and Ruskin. Conrad and Henry James, both of whom befriended Crane, had their own relation to the impressionist mode, and each realized that Crane was a pure or natural impressionist, indeed the only one, according to Conrad.

1

Pater, deftly countering Matthew Arnold, stated the credo of literary impressionism:

> The first step towards seeing one's object as it really is, is to know one's impression as it really is, to discriminate it, to realize it distinctly.

Pater's "object" is a work of art, verbal or visual, but the critic here has stated Stephen Crane's quest to see the object of experience as it is, to know one's impression of it, and to realize that impression in narrative fiction. Scholarly arguments as to whether and to what degree *The Red Badge of Courage* is naturalistic, symbolist, or impressionist, can be set aside quickly. Joyce's *Ulysses* is both naturalistic and symbolist within the general perspective of the Paterian or impressionistic "epiphany" or privileged moment, but juxtapose the *Red Badge* to *Ulysses* and Crane is scarcely naturalistic or symbolist in comparison. Crane is altogether an impressionist, in his "vivid impressionistic description of action on that woodland battlefield," as Conrad phrased it, or, again in Conrad's wording, in "the imaginative analysis of his own temperament tried by the emotions of a battlefield."

If Crane's impressionism had a single literary origin, as to some extent is almost inevitable, Kipling is that likely forerunner. The puzzles of literary ancestry are most ironical here, since Kipling's precursor was Mark Twain. Hemingway's famous observation that all modern American literature comes out of the one book *Huckleberry Finn* is only true of Crane, the indubitable beginning of our modern literature, insofar as Crane took from Kipling precisely what the author of *The Light That Failed* and *Kim* owed to Twain. Michael Fried's association of Crane with the painter Eakins is peculiarly persuasive, since Crane's visual impressionism is so oddly American, without much resembling Whistler's. Crane is almost the archetype of the writer as a child of experience, yet I think this tends to mean that then there are a few strong artistic precursors, rather than a tradition that makes itself available. Associate Crane with Kipling and Eakins, on the way to, but still a distance from, Conrad and the French Post-Impressionists, and you probably have stationed him accurately enough.

II

The Red Badge of Courage is necessarily a story about fear. Crane's Young Soldier, again as Conrad noted, "dreads not danger but fear itself. . . . In this he stands for the symbol of all untried men." Henry Fleming, as eventually we come to know the Young Soldier, moves ironically from a dangerous self-doubt to what may be an even more dangerous dignity. This is the novel's famous yet perhaps equivocal conclusion:

> For a time this pursuing recollection of the tattered man took all elation from the youth's veins. He saw his vivid error, and he was afraid that it would stand before him all his life. He took no share in the chatter of his comrades, nor did he look at them or know them, save when he felt sudden suspicion that they were seeing his thoughts and scrutinizing each detail of the scene with the tattered soldier.
>
> Yet gradually he mustered force to put the sin at a distance. And at last his eyes seemed to open to some new ways. He found that he could look back upon the brass and bombast of his earlier gospels and see them truly. He was gleeful when he discovered that he now despised them.
>
> With this conviction came a store of assurance. He felt a quiet manhood, nonassertive but of sturdy and strong blood. He knew that he would no more quail before his guides wherever they should point. He had been to touch the great death, and found that, after all, it was but the great death. He was a man.
>
> So it came to pass that as he trudged from the place of blood and wrath his soul changed. He came from hot plowshares to prospects of clover tranquilly, and it was as if hot plowshares were not. Scars faded as flowers.
>
> It rained. The procession of weary soldiers became a bedraggled train, despondent and muttering, marching with churning effort in a trough of liquid brown mud under a low, wretched sky. Yet the youth smiled, for he saw that the world was a world for him, though many discovered it to be made of oaths and walking sticks. He had rid himself of the red sickness of battle. The sultry nightmare was in the past. He had been an animal blistered and sweating in the heat and pain of war. He turned now with a lover's thirst to images of tranquil skies, fresh meadows, cool brooks— an existence of soft and eternal peace.
>
> Over the river a golden ray of sun came through the hosts of leaden rain clouds.

More Hemingway than Hemingway is that very American sentence: "He had been to touch the great death, and found that, after all, it was but the great death. He was a man." Is the irony of that dialectical enough to suffice? In context, the power of the irony is beyond question, since Crane's prose is strong enough to bear rephrasing as: "He had been to touch the great fear, and found that, after all, it was still the great fear. He was not yet a man." Crane's saving nuance is that the fear of being afraid dehumanizes, while accepting one's own mortality bestows upon one the association with others that grants the dignity of the human. How does Crane's prose find the strength to sustain a vision that primary and normative? The answer, I suspect, is the Bible and Bunyan, both of them being deeply at work in this unbelieving son of a Methodist minister: "He came from hot plowshares to prospects of clover tranquilly, and it was as if hot plowshares were not." The great trope of Isaiah is assimilated in the homely and unassuming manner of Bunyan, and we see the Young Soldier, Henry Fleming, as an American Pilgrim, anticipating when both sides of the Civil War "shall beat their swords into plowshares, and their spears into pruning hooks."

III

Crane's accurate apprehension of the phantasmagoria that is battle has been compared to Tolstoy's. There is something to such a parallel, perhaps because Tolstoy even more massively is a biblical writer. What is uniquely Crane's, what parts him from all prior visionaries of warfare, is difficult to define, but is of the highest importance for establishing his astonishing originality. Many examples might be chosen, but I give the death of the color sergeant from the conclusion of chapter 19:

> Over the field went the scurrying mass. It was a handful of men splattered into the faces of the enemy. Toward it instantly sprang the yellow tongues. A vast quantity of blue smoke hung before them. A mighty banging made ears valueless.
>
> The youth ran like a madman to reach the woods before a bullet could discover him. He ducked his head low, like a football player. In his haste his eyes almost closed, and the scene was a wild blur. Pulsating saliva stood at the corners of his mouth.
>
> Within him, as he hurled himself forward, was born a love, a despairing fondness for this flag which was near him. It was a creation of beauty and invulnerability. It was a goddess, radiant, that bended its form with an imperious gesture to him. It was a woman, red and white, hating and loving, that called him with the voice of his hopes. Because no harm could come to it he endowed it with power. He kept near, as if it could be a saver of lives, and an imploring cry went from his mind.

In the mad scramble he was aware that the color sergeant flinched suddenly, as if struck by a bludgeon. He faltered, and then became motionless, save for his quivering knees.

He made a spring and a clutch at the pole. At the same instant his friend grabbed it from the other side. They jerked at it, stout and furious, but the color sergeant was dead, and the corpse would not relinquish its trust. For a moment there was a grim encounter. The dead man, swinging with bended back, seemed to be obstinately tugging, in ludicrous and awful ways, for the possession of the flag.

It was past in an instant of time. They wrenched the flag furiously from the dead man, and, as they turned again, the corpse swayed forward with bowed head. One arm swung high, and the curved hand fell with heavy protest on the friend's unheeding shoulder.

In the "wild blur" of this phantasmagoria, there are two images of pathos, the flag and the corpse of the color sergeant. Are they not to some degree assimilated to one another, so that the corpse becomes a flagpole, and the flag a corpse? Yet so dialectical is the interplay of Crane's biblical irony that the assimilation, however incomplete, itself constitutes a figure of doubt as to the normative intensities of patriotism and group solidarity that the scene exemplifies, both in the consciousness of Henry Fleming and in that of the rapt reader. The "despairing fondness" for the flag is both a Platonic and a Freudian Eros, but finally more Freudian. It possesses "invulnerability" for which the soldier under fire has that Platonic desire for what he himself does not possess and quite desperately needs, but it manifests even more a Freudian sense of the ambivalence both of and towards the woman as object of the drive, at once a radiant goddess sexually bending her form though imperiously, yet also a woman, red and white, hating and loving, destroying and healing.

The corpse of the color sergeant, an emblem of devotion to the flag and the group even beyond death, nevertheless keeps Fleming and his friend from the possibility of survival as men, compelling them to clutch and jerk at the pole, stout and furious. Life-in-death incarnate, the corpse obstinately tugs for the staff of its lost life. Homer surely would have appreciated the extraordinary closing gesture, as the corpse sways forward, head bowed but arm swung high for a final stroke, as "the curved hand fell with heavy protest on the friend's unheeding shoulder."

Crane is hardly the American Homer; Walt Whitman occupies that place forever. Still, *The Red Badge of Courage* is certainly the most Homeric prose narrative ever written by an American. One wants to salute it with Whitman's most Homeric trope, when he says of the grass:

And now it seems to me the beautiful uncut hair of graves.

JOHN BERRYMAN

The Color of This Soul

His friends while he was alive and his critics since have found Stephen Crane mysterious, inscrutable. Every reader has observed the ghastly reign in his work of the color Red and the emotion Fear. I once tried to puzzle out the relation between them, and coming back to Thomas Beer's book after a long time I was electrified: "Let it be stated that the mistress of this boy's mind was fear. His search in aesthetic was governed by terror as that of tamer men is governed by the desire of women." The first sentence seems now to be famous. It is cited by the account of Crane in the recent *Literary History of the United States,* which then goes on, implausibly enough, to speak of the "simple facts" of Crane's life, "the familiar story of romantic youth," "an almost classic formula," but is presently confessing that "the sources of Crane's philosophy and art are as yet undeciphered." "Simple" and "familiar" are not the words that would have occurred to one, though there may indeed turn out to be something classic in this life. It is better to recognize an enigma, as the author of this very fair new account then does.

The nature of the enigma was declared with precision by Mark Van Doren, twenty-five years ago, when he remarked that the compliment that would eventually be paid Crane "will take the form of an analysis of his need to live, at least as an artist, in the midst of all but unbearable excitement." We have now seen this excitement also in Crane's life, a fury of writing and action, coupled with an extraordinary personal silence, a mystery of inertia and sudden rebellious movement, hopeless tentative loves, a discontinuous kindness of life and wild cruelty of art, obsession with dogs and horses, with babies, with older women, with whores, obsession with death. Our impression

From *Stephen Crane.* © 1950 by William Sloane Associates. Meridian Books, 1962.

is undoubtedly chaotic. Still, certain elements emerge distinct and strange, among them perhaps above all those associated with prostitutes and with war. Why was Stephen Crane obliged to champion prostitutes? Why was he obliged to spend his life imagining and seeking war? Perhaps no answers to these questions are to be had, but there seems no reason to suppose so until we have tried to answer them—as warily and also as boldly as need be. Let me say at this point that we are not in quest of *reasons* for Crane's greatness as an artist. I suspect that no explanation is available for greatness. All we can hope to see, with luck, care, time, labor and devotion, is *where it comes from. Why* it comes is another matter. Taking as a starting point the first of the two crucial questions just posed, what can we learn?

Ten years after Crane's death a Viennese student of the human mind published a dozen pages on "A Special Type of Choice of Objects Made by Men," attempting to account for an anomaly encountered repeatedly by him in psychiatric practice. Therapy was not an issue; the paper sought a general psychological explanation of certain very curious observed facts. The problem Freud set himself was to account for the juxtaposition in certain men of a disconcerting series of "conditions of love." He found four conditions. The woman loved must involve, first, an "injured third party"—some other man, that is, who has a right of possession, as husband or betrothed or near friend. She must be, second, "more or less sexually discredited"—"within the limits of a significant series" from a married woman known to be flirtatious up to an actual harlot; "love for a harlot" Freud called this condition. Third, this highly compulsive situation is repeated, with sincerity and intensity repeated; even, in consequence of external conditions (such as changes of residence and environment), to a long chain of such experiences. Fourth: "The trait in this type of lover that is most astonishing to the observer is the desire they express to 'rescue' the beloved."

Now though our knowledge of Stephen Crane's life is incomplete and in part uncertain, one or two of these "conditions" are immediately striking as characteristic of it: the "love for a harlot," and the "injured third party" (Cora Stewart's husband). It ought to be worthwhile to investigate the extent to which they are characteristic, and whether Freud's other conditions are present also. I must emphasize at once the fact that we are dealing mainly with *unconscious* compulsion. Depending upon temperament, strength of personal character, and circumstances, such compulsion issues or does not issue into consciousness or into action. We are interested not only in what Stephen Crane *did* but in what we find there is evidence that he was compelled toward. It is not here suggested that Crane knew his compulsions or felt, for instance, any conscious wish to "injure" a "third party."

The condition of an "injured third party" is certain in his common-law marriage. Mrs. Munroe or "L.B.," earlier, although unhappy with her husband, was married. Writing to a friend about Miss Crouse, Crane mentions someone's "rivals" for her; of whom he became tentatively one. Helen Trent was engaged to be married, but Crane (according to Beer) did not know this and withdrew immediately he learned it; the elderly lady she companioned falls within Freud's ground. Of Amy Leslie's situation, apart from the fact that her first husband had died, we know nothing, nor of early loves except that the Canadian lady with seven children was no doubt married.

His relation with Cora, and an exceptional concern with prostitutes, must probably establish the second condition; but within the "discredited" range falls also Amy Leslie, an ex-actress.

The recurrences with which we have been dealing go far to establish the third condition also—including one to come. For a life so absorbed and short, one certainly hears of many loves. It must be mentioned as significant—dealing, I repeat, with unconscious compulsion—that with Crane's only change of environment after he married, the journey to Cuba, we hear of a widow in whose lodging house he stayed, writing, long after even Beer remarks that he should have returned to England; she is said to have mothered him, insisting on his eating reasonably and taking a walk at night; her portrait in "His Majestic Lie" is devoted. But if the three long letters written to Cora and now announced for early publication are genuine, the slight doubt attaching to this third "condition" disappears: they are said, weirdly enough, to describe to her "his European amatory adventures."

Of the desire to "rescue" the beloved, enough has been said in earlier chapters. His appearance in court and Cora's prose-poem alone would do. But it has great interest that this last condition of the four appears to stand, Freud wrote, "merely in a loose and superficial relation, founded entirely on conscious grounds, to these phantasies that have gained control of the love-experiences of real life." The rescue theme, therefore, in life (Dora Clark, Doris Watts, Cora Taylor) was able *consciously*, no doubt, to imitate the rescue-action of his mother in regard to the fallen woman which he consciously remembered; and this theme is often, as we have seen, undisguised in his writing. This is the first time we have had occasion to allude to Crane's mother and almost the only time she will occur in a context *conscious* to Crane.

The life thus seems to display with perfect distinctness all four of the conditions that puzzled Freud. This great scientist observed carefully at the close of his paper that his aim in it had been simply "first of all to single out extreme types in sharp outline . . . there is a far greater number of persons in whom only one or two of the typical features, and even these but indistinctly traced, are recognizable." Crane strikes one then as decidedly "an extreme type in sharp outline." The paper reads indeed, upon sufficient exploration, like a study of Crane, and its immense insight receives from Crane's life and work decisive confirmation. But one major point remains to be noticed. It is required, in elaboration of the second condition, that jealousy accompany the valuing of the love-object—not jealousy of the "injured third party," strangely, but jealousy of new acquaintances or friends in regard to whom the woman may be brought under suspicion. Now we know little enough about Crane's relation with his wife (or any other woman), but one friend who did and whom the record has let speak is definite. On gossip concerning Mrs. Crane early in 1900, Robert Barr wrote that Crane "is subject to a kind of jealousy that knows how to hurt him worst." In the absence of any but this witness, evidence from Crane's writing may be given weight. In his three long novels jealousy as we have seen is dominant, not only of the heroes' chief rivals (Oglethorpe, Coke, Forister) but of others. In "The Clan of No Name," Mr. Smith sits waiting with a dull fear of the girl's having gone off with one of his "dream-rivals. . . . It was part of his love to believe in the absolute treachery of his adored one." In the third story dealing with two Kids, "A Man by the Name of Mud," one Kid is infatuated, again with a light woman (chorus girl) and behaves with brilliant indifference until, at the very end: "Wants to be dead sure there are no others. Once suspects it, and immediately makes the colossal mistake of his life. Takes the girl to task. Girl won't stand it for a minute. Harangues him. Kid surrenders and pleads with her—pleads with her. Kid's name is mud." The exact coincidence, finally, of parts of "Intrigue" with Freud's formula may be taken as conclusive.

> Beware of my friends,
> Be not in speech too civil,
> For in all courtesy
> My weak heart sees spectres,
> Mists of desire
> Arising from the lips of my chosen;
> Be not civil.

The whole case, in fine, displays itself as classical, and the peculiar urgency of certain of these "conditions" for Stephen Crane is realized when we recall emotions out of his life: his startling excitement, for instance, over the necessity of *rescuing* Helen Trent from a rather abstract association which to her was nothing, to us seems nothing, and to Crane was all-important because it was capable of being regarded as *discreditable*.

The explanation of the type at which Freud arrived will perhaps, after forty years, surprise few of my readers, so familiar has time made us with two or three of his basic concepts. But this familiarity, fortunate so far as it has weakened our denying sense of shock, is very unfortunate so far as it can make us glib. It might be better to attend as to a matter wholly new, profoundly incongruous and difficult. The type, Freud said, is that in which "the libido has dwelt so long in its attachment to the mother, even after puberty, that the maternal characteristics remain stamped on the love-objects chosen later—so long that they all become easily recognizable mother surrogates." Following the revelation to a boy of the secret of sexual life, especially and incredibly as he applies it to his parents, and the further revelation of women who are said to be for hire and are despised (and now shudderingly longed for), the boy performs the cynical identification of mother and harlot: "they both do the same thing." Much earlier desires are reactivated, and he "comes, as we say, under the sway of the Oedipus complex": he begins to desire the mother, hates the father for standing in his way, and regards the mother as unfaithful to him with the father. Fantasies of the mother's infidelity, in which the lover bears his image, serve to gratify both desire and revenge; and fixation upon these fantasies produces the "harlot" as a surrogate. Thus the second "condition." In the first, the "injured third party" is simply the father himself. The repetition or series—Freud's third condition—resolves the pressing desire in the unconscious for what is irreplaceable, the "one" mother: she must be sought again and again (though in a fidelity each time sincere) since the satisfaction longed for is never found. "Rescue" is complex. Her propensity to infidelity means that the loved one must be watched and protected. But the "saving" of the mother, who gave the boy life, is by a shift to give her back another life, that is, a child, a child as like himself as possible—and this involves an identification of himself with the father. Fantasies of rescuing the father are usually defiant ("I want nothing from him; I repay him all I have cost him"). In rescue of the mother, however, "All the instincts, the loving, the grateful, the sensual, the defiant, the self-assertive and independent—all are gratified in the wish to be the father of himself." A fixation upon this fantasy, in the compulsive "rescue" of (degraded) mother-surrogates, then gratifies, obviously, powerful instincts; and one of Stephen Crane's most puzzling habits begins to make sense.

What have we learned? Something: that although Crane's situation in the type is special—a genius, bearing an historic name, the last child of a large family and a minister's, with a dominant mother, a widow's son early "deserted" by his father and left poor, dependent upon his brothers, and so on—there exists all the same a definite type of psychic life in which he is a case. He becomes *less* mysterious, at any rate; and certain things large and small in his life we can understand. We understand better, for instance, why he married a woman in the situation of Cora Taylor. It was a chance for rescue. The conversation Robert Davis witnessed with the girl on Broadway in 1897, related by Davis nearly thirty years later, is now really guaranteed: "I can show you the way out." The choice of the subject of *Maggie,* his first work, following immediately upon his mother's death, is less mysterious: it gave him a chance for rescue, he could show Maggie the way out. (The way out was death, and we shall return to this.) Light is thrown on the ambivalence of Crane's attitude toward women—on the one hand, his special attentiveness to older women (Helen Trent and earlier the Canadian woman, Mrs. Munroe, Mrs. Chaffee and Mrs. Sonntag, Amy Leslie, Cora Taylor, Mary Horan), and on the other hand his obvious misogyny, expressed in the Claverack society S(ic) S(emper) T(yrannis) Girlum, in hatred of society matrons and women on porches, in the extreme fear his heroes show of the girls they love, in wild aggression against one mother (made drunken and cruel) in *Maggie* and the over-solicitous, virtuous *George's Mother,* the first shown driving her daughter into the street, the second shown driven by her son to death. The pattern of simultaneous desire, nervous loathing, and resentment described by Freud is recognizable again and again. When in *Maggie* Mrs. Johnson whirls her great fist in grown Jimmie's face: "He threw out his left hand and writhed his fingers about her middle arm. The mother and the son began to sway and struggle." But the general war upon Authority in Crane's life and art we can look to find rooted rather in jealousy and hatred of the father, when we have come finally round to that.

Let us begin as simply as possible with the notion of a mind at formidable tension, in an acute form of the human predicament with regard to parents. We have called a major aspect of this tension Fear. Fear, I suppose, is a response to danger. Now it is a singular fact that there is not very much danger in Crane's work. There is a great deal of something else, which let us call menace: an abstract form of danger, the possibility of fatal intervention. Menace is everywhere at all times in life, only most of us do not feel it, luckily. Crane felt it. With what sort of fear did he respond? He has reckoned certainly with every stage of this emotion, but few readers will doubt that at his most characteristic it is Panic. In "An Illusion in Red and White," for instance, the boy's mind "began to work like ketchup" under his terrible vision of his mother's murderer. The word is itself rather frequent in Crane,—at the outset of *The Red Badge,* "A little panic-fear grew" in the hero's mind wondering whether he will run away. But panic is not so directly a form of fear as it is an overwhelming form of anxiety, where control has failed and a regression occurs, driving the emotion back behind the point at which particular danger is occurring, toward an earlier general terror: toward what is called a trauma. As a response, that is, it exceeds any possible fear that can be felt for any conceivable particular danger, because it opens again some ancient vista.

Though panic has various situations in Crane, its situation as a rule is War. What can we make of this? Crane had never seen any war, and was only in the ordinary way familiar with the notion of war, when his feeling about it *possessed* him forever. Now in men whose Oedipus complex has persisted, the love-object is valued (unconsciously) because it can stand for the mother. So with other valued objects and activities: they may be representatives of dominating earlier objects and activities. Perhaps war is a representative. If so, it will represent a conflict of some kind. But let us put his situation (or subject) and his emotion together, or, more precisely, his obsession and his anxiety together. What early conflict is it that will produce a panic which, apparently forgotten, can rule a life?

I am thinking not so much of the so-called "primal scene" itself just here, as of what are known as primal-scene substitutes. These are observations of animals or adults, or of scenes even that may not objectively be sexual at all but that are experienced as sexual by the child—transferring themselves, under circumstantial similarities, and with powerful effect, to the unconscious memory of the "primal scene" proper. At the age of twelve, he "saw a white girl stabbed by her Negro lover" (I am quoting Beer, whose source I have not found—probably Willis Clarke's interview with Crane) "on the edge of a road-maker's camp. He galloped the pony home and said nothing to Mrs. Crane although he was sweating with fright." It is a remarkable scene, and so is the silence, even though his mother had taught him to be "brave." If the incident can really show a relation with themes in Crane's art, perhaps we have found what we were looking for.

Examples of Negroes or Africa as a symbol—a natural one—for "darkness" and "sex" and "sin" come readily to mind. Crane's earliest signed sketch eulogizes an *explorer* of Africa. The destroyed story "Vashti in the Dark" told, we recall, "how a young *Methodist preacher* from the South killed himself after discovering that his wife had been ravished by a Negro in a *forest* at *night*"; and we have seen a Crane-mask in the Negro rescuer who becomes a "monster." But let us examine in detail his first published story, "The King's Favor." A promising New York tenor sings before an African king, is acclaimed a great warrior and is offered the honor of one of the king's wives, who stands six feet two; frightened, he offers the king, in order to propitiate him for not accepting her, a most suspicious collection of objects: an umbrella, suspenders, playing cards, a pistol, a knife, and so on. These are familiar, in fact, as phallic symbols and taken together with the other materials of this curious story make it hard to suppose that we have not here a sort of telescoping of the primal-scene substitute and the persisting Oedipal situation. The libido, wanting the mother, actually arranges for the father to offer her; but fantasy renders the acceptance as a rejection, the offering of symbols as "propitiation." The wife is made immense partly to satisfy the mother-image and partly to supply a ground for refusing her. But even more striking than the fact that the father is here imagined as an inhabitant of the attractive Dark Continent is the means employed by the intruder to win his favor and thus the offer of his wife. The tenor sings a *war*-song.

Little as we are yet equipped to assemble all these themes, let us see where this sudden, crucial introduction of War leads. Crane's original artistic interest was not just in war but intensely in the *Civil War*. He had already written *Maggie,* the subject of which is civil war in a slum family: parents against children and against each other, son striking daughter, son and mother wrestling, mother cursing and ruining daughter—the room is a scene of continual riot, blows, destruction, and Crane's language is *military*. Jimmie hiding on the stairway "heard howls and curses, groans and shrieks—a confused chorus as if a battle were raging." Even the public fight between Jimmie with his friend and Pete is civil, since these two have been comrades in thuggery, and their faces too "now began to fade to the pallor of warriors in the blood and heat of a battle." A predisposition toward war plainly was strong. The Civil War was the last war, the one heard about and mimicked; we have seen the child Stephen playing war games. But we lack still a direct connection backward with the Negro stabbing or the story of the African's "favor." Perhaps this is to be found in the fact that the Civil War was precisely *about the Negro*—about the object, that is, of Crane's own (fantasied) horror, envy, fascination, and inquiry. Driven to imagine repeatedly the feelings of boys and men panic-stricken, he took the natural line to the Civil War; but the point is that he seems to have taken it *compulsively*, obeying a bond, and once he had fastened upon the Civil War he left it chiefly to find representatives of it in other wars visited and imagined. It was no casual or accidental absorption that produced the greatest American novel about that war.

But the nexus Negro-War is wholly censored in *The Red Badge of Courage,* and so the present account had better be regarded as provisional until we come to further evidence of a different kind. Only two confirmations may be touched, one outside the novel and one in it. At the moments in Crane's work, first, where stabbing is in question, a Negro is always suggested with less or more distinctness in the context, and his latest one was openly of war. Reserving two examples, I shall give only that now with one introductory to it pitched very high indeed in tone.

When the New York Kid is confronted in a Mexican street, "fascinated, stupified, he actually watched the progress of the man's thought toward the point where a knife would be wrenched from its sheath. . . . The emotion, a sort of mechanical fury . . . smote the *dark* contenance in wave after wave"; and "dark countenance" is more explicit at the death of the Cuban lieutenant with his stunning new machete in "The Clan of No Name": he lies wounded, a man comes to kill him having a "*negro* face," they exchange a "singular" glance, and the lieutenant "closed his eyes, for he did not want to see the flash of the machete."

Then as to the mother and *The Red Badge of Courage*. To make the mother sorry is a form of punishment; it leads also to renewed favor. The hero's leaving his mother is detailed with care, and even though it falls below his expectations— "He had privately primed himself for a beautiful scene" —her face at last is stained with tears (so that he goes off "suddenly ashamed"). This ambivalent theme is more undisguised still in "His New Mittens": "He would run away. In a remote corner of the world he would become some sort of bloody-handed person driven to a life of crime by the barbarity of his mother. . . . He would torture her for years with doubts and doubts, and drive her implacably to a repentant grave." This boy, whose sins against his mother began in a "delirium of snow-battle," does not get far before he is taken home by the butcher (an intimate friend of his dead father's) and "Upon a couch Horace saw his mother lying limp, pale as death, her eyes gleaming with pain." It can scarcely be coincidence that Kelcey of *George's Mother* is summoned home from a fight to witness his mother's death (for which his degradation is responsible). The impression one receives from these works is that in *The Red Badge* too the unconscious motive is to disquiet and woo— as with a war-song—the mother-image. All three appear to display, in their degrees, the Oedipal resentment-and-craving thrown into fantastic activity.

The father is dead in them, as in *Maggie* drinking and swearing he dies early, George's "fell off a scaffoldin'," Henry Fleming's "never drunk a drop of licker in his life, and seldom swore a cross oath," and this is all we know of them. But it is time to come directly to the father-image, against whom aggression is as remarkable in all this work as the author's reverence for his father was in life, and we can best approach this crucial, difficult subject through a consideration of some of the ways in which Stephen Crane represented himself in his art.

The *names* authors give their characters have seldom received sufficient attention unless the significance of a name is immediately striking, as in certain thousands from Marina and Perdita down to Princess Volupine (a syncopation of "voluptuous, lupine"). These are deliberate, conscious. So as a rule are

Henry James's: everyone has noticed Mrs. Grose, whose perceptions are less
"fine" than those of the nameless governess in "The Turn of the Screw," but
it was pointed out only last year that the children's names are symbolic (Flora
and Miles, for flower and soldier), and perhaps other names are, like Bly and
Quint. Often the naming is less clearly conscious, though strongly patterned.
Frank Norris's biographer notices, without attempting to explain it, his habit
of giving masculine names to his women characters: Lloyd, Turner, Sidney,
Page, Travis; his daughter Jeannette he called only Billy. Now Crane could
be adroit on occasion with names. Corwin Linson he made into "Corinson,"
Acton Davies into "Shackles." But beyond these definite instances I shall not
attempt to judge how far the habits of naming we are to study were *conscious*
in Crane. In all likelihood many were partly so, but since the drives they
illustrate in the personality were mainly unconscious speculation is futile.

And the first great fact we come on is the *absence* of names—a compulsive namelessness. Transposing the Crane family, fantasied and altered,
into an Irish slum-family, he refuses to give the characters any names, and
he will not give his name as the author. As the "little man" of the Sullivan
County sketches, he usually has no name. Two of his main heroes have no
name, the correspondent in "The Open Boat" and the Swede in "The Blue
Hotel." When for three stories he apparently split himself into the New York
Kid and the San Francisco Kid, both are nameless. Even after he taught himself
to use names, his reluctance to divulge them is very great. . . . He loved to
confuse names. The two Colonel Butlers opposing each other in "Ol' Ben-
net" are historical but he clearly enjoys them, and in one of the later, careful
pieces about Timothy Lean ("The Upturned Face") we read: "Lean looked
at his two men. 'Attention,' he barked. The privates came to attention with
a click, looking much aggrieved. The adjutant lowered his helmet to his knee.
Lean, bareheaded, he stood over the grave." Another instance of confusion
more startling [can be seen] in "The Blue Hotel."

Some inhibition affecting the name "Crane" and then names in general
must be at work, and we may suppose it a consequence of the Oedipal guilt-
sense toward the father, whose place he wishes to take with the mother. But
there is probably some self-consolation present also ("If I am not a Crane,
my desire is not forbidden"), and some *defiance* (obliteration of the father's
sign in him, the patronym). It is relevant that Crane fantasied a daughter for
himself, "little Cora," not a son who would continue to bear the name, and
fantasied a daughter so strongly that he can remark casually in "War
Memories," "If I had been the father of a hundred suffering daughters . . ."
The defiance is more evident still in his insisting, when he has to take names,
on taking *common* names, the commonest possible. For the historic name

Stephen Crane, he takes "Johnson Smith" —which an error altered to "Johnston Smith" —and all three of these names recur, because Crane learned to use names for his purpose. He thought no doubt that he was picking names at random, but I am speaking of what his imagination learned and did.

The first hero of this antiheroic author was the African explorer Henry Stanley. Henry is the name of the hero of *The Red Badge of Courage*, the name of "The Monster," and the name displaced at the catastrophe of "The Blue Hotel," and we shall come shortly to a prince Henry. It is time to mention that Stephen Crane seems to have had a middle name beginning with "H" which he dropped after 1893, and perhaps it was "Henry" —a name very common in the family. Not even the name Stanley disappears.

The second hero of this antiheroic author was the tenor Albert G. Thies. This man sang at Claverack the year before he was put in a story; I do not suppose he had been to Africa, but Crane sent him there to sing a war-song. How conscious Crane was of being a tenor we discover from allusions in the *Pike County Puzzle*, *The Black Riders* (2), *War Is Kind* (16)—all ironic.

> There was a man with tongue of wood
> Who essayed to sing,
> And in truth it was lamentable.

In the last chapter of *The Third Violet*, the hero says to the girl, "I didn't mean to act like a tenor," and later, "I suppose, after all, I did feel a trifle like a tenor when I first came here, but you have chilled it all out of me." We recall Crane's curious habit of humming with his face close to the strings of a violin; he liked to strum on a guitar, and no doubt he plucked the strings of the violin, and it is time to say what he seems to have been thinking of: he seems to have been thinking of war. A number of passages about the sound of bullets suggest this odd conclusion, but one in "The Price of the Harness" seems to enforce it: "as these were mainly high shots it was usual for them to make the faint note of a vibrant string, touched elusively, half-dreamily." He was dreaming of war, or dreaming of love, a war-song. But what are we to make now of this tangle of music and war, desire, this tenor and Africa? It is hard to suppose that Albert G. Thies seized the boy's imagination just as a tenor sufficiently to be dispatched as a Crane-representative to the strange land where the father-image is king. Certainly this may have occurred but we shall need to know why in order to believe it.

Thies is an odd name. In various spellings it occurs in all of the Scandinavian countries, Holland, Germany. Perhaps Crane fixed it as Swedish, though doubtfully, but at any rate this cluster of associations must have stirred him considerably, for it seems to explain a succession of allusions in his work otherwise absolutely mystifying. *Fleming* as a name for the hero of *The Red Badge* is not mystifying, but *Hollanden* for the young writer (the secondary Crane-representative) in *The Third Violet* is a little, as it is that one of Crane's major heroes should be nameless Swede. We recall suddenly a mysterious conversation downstairs in the Blue Hotel about whether this Swede is a Swede after all or "some kind of a Dutchman" —Mr. Blanc the easterner refusing to decide. But this conversation is no longer mysterious: the characters are arguing out some problem of Crane's. When to "Fleming" we add "Hollander" (made Hollanden), this uncertain talk of a Swede or "Dutchman," an imaginary "Prince Henry of Prussia" whom we shall shortly see treating the father-image very differently from Thies, yet another fear-crazed Swede we will encounter at the end, and other evidence to be dealt with at once, the conclusion is inescapable that Thies cannot have set off in Crane's mind this complicated train. Instead he must be simply its first embodiment, and its origin we must seek earlier, in some connection made by Crane (unconsciously) between the Negro with his knife or razor and the Swede or German invading Zululand with his war-song.

These things are difficult. Perhaps the village barber was the link. Whilomville's is called "Reifsnyder" in "The Monster" and "Neeltje" in "The Angel Child," names suggestive indeed, in this context and in view of (1) Reifsnyder's almost unique opinion that Henry Johnson ought *not* to be let die, and (2) the cooperation with the dreamy painter of "the utter Neeltje." Whom for that matter except a barber would the boy, terrified by the Negro's stabbing, normally see with a knife or razor? His father shaving (in memory)—and the father-image of "Four Men in a Cave" terrifies the little man by drawing a long thin knife, Trescott in "The Monster" "was shaving this lawn as if it were a priest's chin." The town butcher—and it was actually the butcher, with knife poised and named Stickney, identified as an intimate friend of the dead father, whom we saw conducting home the runaway boy. But some Swedish, Dutch, or German barber seems alone to account for the series of dramatizations beginning with Thies. To the boy acted on by the fantasy of stabbing as a sexual act, all the associations forward to fighting and battle, Negroes and Swedes, backward to the Oedipal fantasies and inhibitions, start alive then with excited relation. A great body of his most powerful and casual-looking metaphor depends upon these. "The song of the razor is seldom heard," he will lament in a vivacious, nostalgic article on Negro killers in Minetta Lane of old. Or the body of the crazy Swede is "pierced as easily as if it had been a melon" —and only at the climax of "The Knife" can we guess what Crane's association was: there come on one another suddenly in a melon patch at night, each with knife ready for theft, two Negroes.

Passing to the grotesque aggression against the father-image of Prince Henry which initiates our final cluster of themes, a word of limitation. Just as very little of the complicated supporting evidence (positive and negative) for even the leading themes of Crane's unconscious thought which I have been following can be given, so a treatise elaborate indeed would be required to distinguish from the Oedipal elements in this aggression against the father, first, the sense of desertion and impoverishment (with the consequent resentments) arising from his death when Crane was a boy, and second, the intellectual rebellion consciously waged by Crane against him. Thus in poems the father-image (sage or seer) is generally on a high place and hypocrisy is the usual charge, suggesting that the original incredulous revulsion on learning that the parent who preaches on Sunday "does it too" is still governing the poet's fantasies. It is remarkable how often *sight* is associated with these poems.

> You say you are holy,
> And that
> Because I have not seen you sin.
> Ay, but there are those
> Who see you sin, my friend.

Sometimes the "I" seems to be identified with the father, the Crane-mask being another, even a devil.

> I stood upon a high place,
> And saw, below, many devils
> Running, leaping,
> And carousing in sin.
> One looked up, grinning,
> And said, "Comrade! Brother!"

But this is very uncertain, whereas from the hermit of "Four Men in a Cave" (who took to drink and ruined his family) to The O'Ruddy's father (who did not leave him any money) there can be no doubt that in many dramatizations the unconscious reproach upon at least one subject is non-Oedipal. So probably with family degradation. For the nineties the Irish stood as—what by another delightful turn of democratic opinion the Jews stand as now—a popular type of social squalor; so that the Johnsons, the Scullys, the Kelceys, and the other Irish into which Crane turned his family are aggressive symbols. His light women are Irish: Florinda O'Connor of *The Third Violet,* Nora

Black of *Active Service*. The Irish are looked on of course by the English in *The O'Ruddy* as barbarians. But an ambivalence is certain here. The O'Ruddy, though eloquent about his father's lying and drinking, is jealous of his father's honor, and the family though penniless and Irish is noble. Perhaps, so mixed are all these feelings, it is only with one or more of three symbols present that we can be confident of Oedipal aggression: knives, rivals, death.

Crane's little fantastic play *The Blood of the Martyr* has three tiny acts, the scene laid in China. Prince Henry of Prussia is extorting railway commissions from the Mandarins by sending missionaries everywhere in the land to be martyred, and he is running out of them. In the first act he tells an aide to get more from Berlin, drill them, "feed them up for a time on broken glass, copies of Xenophon's 'Anabasis' and blood," then turn them loose. The aide reports that the missionary at Yen Hock has appealed for assistance, and Prince Henry orders him sent a box of cigars and his compliments: "Tell him he is the right man in the right place." In act 2 the Mandarins are pondering the question of what a railway concession *is,* when Prince Henry enters to announce that the missionary at Yen Hock has been foully murdered: what about a railway concession? The Mandarins are "very tired" and agree to anything— "We wish to slumber, for all the towers are nodding." In act 3 unfortunately the missionary turns up from Yen Hock—on crutches, minus an ear, foot, and lung, garroted and flayed, but alive. Prince Henry, furious, declares him an unworthy son of Germany and deprives him of the cigars, but sends him to the kitchen for beer. This is the entire action of the play.

This skit on imperialism is not of course what it appears, so far as it appears anything. If the father was once an African king, the son is now a German prince. In the missionary of "Yen Hock," however, we could not be certain of a father-image if it were not the nature of a railway concession. When one mandarin suggests that this is like a tea-junk, another says: "No. It looks more like a horse, only that it is a pale purple in color, and has red eyes." Now Crane had already written the story of a dying dope-fiend named "Yen-Nock Bill" with a voice such that his young friend used to wish "that he was a *horse,* so that he could spring upon the bed and trample him to death." A fantasy-horse, then, to murder in the most violent way possible Yen-Nock Bill and the missionary at Yen Hock. Nothing just like these names have I found; Crane evidently invented them. "Yen" is a passionate craving, associated first with the general aggressive word "knock," then particularly with a horse's ankle, both *striking* words. And Prince Henry, in his moment of triumph when he imagines the missionary dead at Yen Hock, cries out: "Thus do the glorious eagles of Germany soar above their *rivals.*"

Stephen Crane as a horse:—a singular image; and intent ferociously upon his father's death. Both men were specially fond and solicitous of horses. Crane remembered his father's unwillingness even to hurry a horse, and Charles Michelson tells us that though other correspondents changed mounts whenever they could get a better one, Crane "took his for better or worse, until the campaign was over." Horses are above all *kindly* throughout Crane's work, they are continually *being* hurt to his silent agony. Identification and ferocity alike are strange; stranger still as they will relate presently to the death of the mother.

Dreams of the parent's death vision as a rule the death of the parent of the same sex; they represent survivals of very early feelings of rivalry, the girl of the mother, the boy of the father. These feelings were fixated in Crane and are certainly present in fantasies of the father's death—Prince Henry's (displaced) word "rivals" is crucial. Whether they entirely account for them is less clear. Sadism grinds strong in Crane's work, as its counterpart masochism does.

> Torn, miserable, and ashamed of my open sorrow,
> I thought of the thunders that lived in my head,
> And I wished to be an ogre,
> And hale and haul my beloved to a castle,
> And there use the happy cruel one cruelly,
> And make her mourn with my mourning.

We can guess at masochism also in the life, cultivating hardship, collecting and preserving all attacks on his poems, mounting all the premature obituaries in a book which he "greatly treasures." Now the last form of this is suicide-fantasy, as the last form of sadism is the parents' death, both parents'. Death ends the terrible excitement under which he is bound to live, death resolves panic, death is "a way out," a rescue. Perhaps the fantasy of rescue is *not* by any means always concealed under the imaged deaths of both father and mother.

Recalling that it was as a mother-surrogate that Maggie took her author's imagination, at the same time that aggressions against both parents are being discharged in her parents the Johnsons, we shall not be surprised if unconscious identification in Crane's work was often much more complex than a summary study like this one can take explicitly into account. The mother is present twice, that is, in *Maggie*—under Mrs. Crane's name Mary as Mary Johnson, and as the girl who becomes a prostitute. Whether the name Maggie is related to Crane's sister Aggie, or (as Margaret) to the light beloved (Margharita) of "The Clan of No Name" and perhaps the heroine of *Active Service* (Marjorie) whose mother is also named Mary, or even to

the name Mary itself (as especially in the Lady Mary whom The O'Ruddy
adores), is doubtful. But it is very remarkable that the hero of *George's Mother*
loves—vainly— "Maggie Johnson" and imagines "scenes in which he rescued
the girl." Equally remarkable is the use of her *mother's* name for the fallen
girl in the first novel. During Maggie's march to death in the river, which
is telescoped as one walk wherein she meets men progressively more terrible,
two of them address her: "Hi, there, Mary. . . . Brace up, old girl," one says,
and another, "Come, now, old lady." This connection of the "rescue" fantasy
with *water*, in the type of fixation to which Crane belongs, Freud thought
especially significant. Water is a birth symbol: "When in a dream a man rescues
a woman from the water, it means that he makes her a mother," which in
view of the father-identification analyzed early in this chapter "means that
he makes her his own mother." Now Maggie is not being rescued *from* the
water but *to* it—exactly as we are about to see George's mother being. By
some frightening twist, Crane's fantasy had to secure father-identification by
drowning the actual mother-representative.

If the act is clear and the person disguised in *Maggie,* the act is disguised
and the person clear in its companion-work *George's Mother.* George drives
his mother to her death by drinking. This is the whole open plot of the short
novel, though nothing could be more emphatic than George's fantasy about
Maggie Johnson: "He reflected that if he could only get a chance to rescue
her from something, the whole tragedy would speedily unwind." We never
learn the mother's first name. Their Irish name "Kelcey" will be enough for
us shortly. The story is flooded with water-images about her: cleaning the
room, she "came from the sink streaming and bedraggled as if she had crossed
a flooded river," and instead of a representation of her death (in bed) our last
view of her is this: "The little old woman lay still with her eyes closed. On
the table at the head of the bed was a glass containing a water-like medicine.
The reflected lights made a silver star on its side." It is significant perhaps
that her son kills her by *drinking.* But these signs would hardly convince if
it were not for one astounding fact and the astounding passage in which Kelcey
receives on the street from a little boy word that she is "awful sick" (in fact,
dying). Here the actual word occurs, displaced like the murderer's "Henry!"
in "The Blue Hotel." His gang are howling derision at him for attending to
the boy's news, and he mutters: " 'I can't—I don't wanta—I don't *wanta leave
me mother be*—she— ' His words were *drowned* in the chorus of their derision." The fact is, that behind "Kelcey" seems to stand, incredibly enough,
the familiar *Irish water-spirit* in the form of a *horse* who warns of drowning
or *helps to drown*: the kelpy.

The reader's head will not improbably be swimming at this point, but is our alternative explanation for these phenomena (coincidence) really plausible of a mind with the habits of naming and symbolization we have seen in Crane's, dealing entirely now in operations that were unconscious? Skepticism would seem to require us to fall back here and elsewhere on the assumption of a series of coincidences more fantastic even than the operations of the human mind, since we are dealing, not with points selected (to prove some thesis) from a large random body of work, but with themes mysterious and dominant in the most imposing products, as well as some of the most puzzling products, of Crane's art. I have been trying simply to isolate the themes, to display them at crisis, and to trace their sources. We are ready, now that we have seen the horse-symbol associated with both the father's and the mother's death, to move towards its origin. Just one poem in *The Black Riders* involves horses; Crane so valued it that he put it first and called the book after it.

> Black riders came from the sea.
> There was clang and clang of spear and shield,
> And clash and clash of hoof and heel,
> Wild shouts and the wave of hair
> In the rush upon the wind:
> Thus the ride of Sin.

It is a queer little poem and a rather famous one. One wonders what thousands of readers have made of it. The riders seem to be enjoying themselves, the "wave of hair" especially has a sensual look, but the poem is madly warlike, and our passage recently with "Hock" tilts "hoof and heel" into prominence. The second and third lines seem to suggest with great force that *the same kind of things* are clashing with each other. "Riding" is a sensual concept, as well as here an aggressive one, and the whole action is described as "sinful." Beyond these considerations I do not know how much further we could get, except that luckily we know the poem's source. At the age of about four Stephen Crane had a recurrent, terrifying dream of black riders charging up at him from the surf. This dream the poem seems faithfully to represent, with adult addition of the last line. The horses themselves are *suppressed in the poem* as perhaps they were also in the dream. We have black riders on horses, but we do not see the horses. What color, I wonder, were the horses? Combers are *white.* And suddenly we remember that just before the summer of this dream "Stephen was held on a white horse which he remembered twenty years later as a savage beast. But it was no part of Mrs. Crane's theory that a child of hers should be afraid of anything. He was told to stay on the horse and not to be scared."

Just possibly we have reached here the bottom of Crane's mind. To ride the white horse is to gratify the mother, to win her favor. The childish dream of fright persisted, at both conscious and unconscious levels, and attached to itself other symbols and motives. The horse associated itself with water. The sinful rider became black, either before or after the stabbing incident determined the sexuality of the whole constellation. If riding is a conventional sexual symbol, waves traditionally horses of the sea, courage a mother's and life's requirement from everyone, none of these were so in ordinary degree with Crane. With baffling and multiplying power they assembled into the supreme experience of his life, when an open boat rode against the snarling of the crests.

But the horse becomes also an instrument of aggression against the rival, the father, and the fantasies of "trampling" begin. Here we are very close to War again, from two sides. To the earlier analysis of War as a representative of sexual "conflict" must now be added: first, the horse aggressive, a charger, for which the only situation in life is War; and second, courage as a means of gratifying the mother. The obvious situation for the display of courage is War—first he plunged himself as Jimmie into civilian fights (*Maggie*), but for a prolonged display he had to move to *The Red Badge of Courage*. *Therefore* it is a "war-song" that wins the favor, earlier, of the offer of the King's wife, and *The Red Badge* is his war-song. We have seen the making of the mother-image "sorry" in this novel. The "great death" in chapter 9, a height of Crane's early art, seems to image the death of the father.

This "tall soldier," Henry Fleming's friend, is the second most important character. His name "Jim" is also that of the soldier whose death is most remarkable in Crane's later war-writings ("The Price of the Harness"), but is it that of a father-image? We recall that the painter in *The Third Violet* is not jealous only of Oglethorpe but actually of his father, who takes his girl for a ride: "With their heads close together they became so absorbed in their conversation that they seemed to forget the painter. He sat on a log and watched them." Gossip about this ride makes the girl's eyes flash "wrath and defiance." Well, at first this father's name is "ol' Jim" Hawker . . . but later "John" . . . , after Oglethorpe's first name has been revealed: it is "Jem"; so that Hawker's rivals have (but very nervously) the same name, and it is the name of a general Crane-mask in his earliest as his latest work, the boy Jimmie. This brief selection of evidence is intended not to secure conviction about the "tall soldier" but simply to introduce two most surprising circumstances of his death. Marching like a "spectre" along, wounded to death, Jim's only fear is lest he be "*run over*" by the artillery wagons (that is: their horses); Henry "hysterically" cries out that he will guard him, but the tall soldier continues to beg in terror. And his only desire is to get to a certain place for his death: "a little clump of bushes . . . the mystic place of his intentions . . . . there was a resemblance in him to a devotee of a mad religion. . . . he had at last found the place for which he had struggled. . . . He was at the rendezvous." I am not going to analyze the sexual and religious elements here except to add that as "Henry Fleming" pursues him to the place "There was a singular race."

Rivalry against the father, and the wish to *be* the father. The more uncertain our analysis, the more singular Crane's identifications appear. We took Henry Johnson's rescue of the boy Jimmie from the fire in "The Monster," and being punished for his rescue with facelessness and idiocy, though protected absolutely by the father, who is punished for *this* "rescue" by ostracism in the society—we took the Negro's rescue to represent the "rescue" swarming in Crane's mind at the time when he was writing the story, his marriage; and we even saw the name "Cora" displaced and disguised as the one "coral" flame in the father's laboratory during the rescue. Probably this was right. But there must be more present, which is not to be explained so. First, as the Negro rescues the Crane-mask, the boy, he represents not only Crane but Crane's father. The rescue-structure of the story is like a musical development: Jimmie's attempt to rescue the flower, and punishment, Johnson's rescue of him, and punishment, Dr. Trescott's rescue of Johnson, and punishment. But second, a rescue may be a rape, and it is only in this unsatisfactory way that I can understand the extraordinary events in the father's room during the fire. Johnson wails a Negro swamp-wail at the threshold (one recalls what is known of "Vashti in the Dark"). "Then he rushed across the room. An orange-coloured flame leaped like a panther at the lavender trousers. This animal bit deeply into Johnson. There was an explosion at one side, and suddenly before him there reared a delicate, trembling sapphire shape like a fairy lady. With a quiet smile she blocked his path and doomed him and Jimmie." Her talons catch him as he tries to plunge past on her left. He falls on his back. From a jar on the desk a "ruby-red snake-like thing" pours out, coils, swims, and flows at last "directly down into Johnson's upturned face." The father's death, even the father's defiled death, is apparently represented in the story called "The Upturned Face," but what is represented here I am not sure, and it is worth discriminating in this difficult relation between what we do not know and what we do know.

What we can know with some confidence even in "The Monster" is that when the idiot Negro, who formerly cared for the doctor's horse, gibbers about a horse, he does so as if he were the horse: " 'I am taking you to Alek Williams, Henry, and I— ' The figure chuckled again. 'No, 'deed! No, seh! Alek Williams

don' know a hoss!' . . . 'I didn't say anything about horses. I was saying— '
'Hoss? Hoss?' said the quavering voice from these near shadows. 'Hoss? 'Deed
I don' know all erbout a hoss! 'Deed I don't.' . . . " Into Henry Fleming's eyes
in *The Red Badge* "came a look that one can see in the orbs of a jaded horse."
Even Crane's conversation shows the obsession: "Say, when I planted those
hoofs of mine on Greek soil . . . " One wonders with pain, at last, just what
form he has—animal or man—in his dying words to Barr: "Robert—when
you come to the hedge—that we must all go over— "

Another thing that we can know, and it must be the end, is that the hero
of *The Red Badge of Courage* and the victim of "The Blue Hotel" meet—
these two characters *meet*, Henry Fleming rescues the Swede and the Swede
dooms Henry Fleming—in a passionate story written midway between these
masterworks. The aggression against the father, the wish to be the father,
and the solution for panic. Is Henry Fleming now both Stephen and the
Reverend Mr. Crane? It is long after the Civil War for "The Veteran," he is
old now, a hero. When he explains that he was afraid at that time, no one
believes him. A hired man, a Swede, drunk, sets the barn afire, and screams,
a "maniac." Old Fleming had been telling the men that young Jim Conklin
"went into it from the start just as if he was born to it. But with me it was
different. I had to get used to it." "I think Steve was born a coward," a friend
of Stephen Crane's told me last year, "but he wouldn't stay one." Old Fleming
was used to it now: entering the inferno, he "took five horses out, and then
came out himself, with his clothes bravely on fire. He had no whiskers, and
very little hair on his head. . . . Some one noticed at the time that he ran
very lamely, *as if one of the frenzied horses had smashed his hip.*" He saves
then the paralyzed Swede. The long flames sing. "And then came this Swede
again, crying as one who is the weapon of the sinister fates. 'De colts! De
colts! You have forgot de colts!' Old Fleming staggered. It was true. . . . 'I
must try to get 'em out.' " The men exclaim: " 'Why, it's suicide for a man
to go in there!' Old Fleming stared absent-mindedly at the open doors. 'The
poor little things!' he said. He rushed into the barn.

> When the roof fell in, a great funnel of smoke swarmed toward
> the sky, as if the old man's mighty spirit, released from its body—a
> little bottle—had swelled like the genie of fable. The smoke was
> tinted rose-hue from the flames, and perhaps the unutterable
> midnights of the universe will have no power to daunt the colour
> of this soul.

DANIEL   G.   HOFFMAN

Love on Earth

Destined to suffer in an indifferent or hostile universe, exiled by sin from the fellowship of the innocent, what solace for the individual can Crane's dark fatalism propose? Recognizing that all sinful mankind is fallen too, he sees the love of another sinful creature as an ideal to be affirmed despite the coldness of God. In the blasted wilderness of our life we may yet find love. But this human love, this cleaving of two sinners in "a reptile-swarming place," is for Crane determined by somewhat unusual circumstances and choices, and it imposes upon the lover an ideal code not only of devotion but of loyalty. This code is not easy to live up to, for lover and beloved alike are menaced by their own fallen, fallible natures. This human love, so passionately desired, so difficult to live, will in the end prove a redemptory principle in Crane's moral universe. But Stephen Crane habitually sought as ministering spirits to his soul's redemption women who seemed to others the least likely consorts to beatitude the world could offer him.

John Berryman has a theory about the persistence of Crane's amatory adventures, which had, to be sure, some rather outlandish patterns. Crane was again and again attracted to older women, usually married, often of questionable reputation—a Canadian mother of seven, an ex-actress, another man's mistress, two chorus girls, a streetwalker, a madame. He was in fact obsessive in his attention to prostitutes, both in life and in his writings. The remarkable point of this interest is his desire to *rescue* them. Mr. Berryman's theory attempts to explain all this, and more: it tells us, too, why he was "obliged to spend his life imagining and seeking war," and tries to show us where Crane's

From *The Poetry of Stephen Crane.* © 1956 by Columbia University Press.

greatness as an artist came from; yet Berryman is careful to make the distinction that for greatness itself "no explanation is available." But the poems Crane wrote of love, his biographer's theory, and its application to this verse must wait until we have set down some necessary biographical information.

Robert H. Davis, a journalist who knew Crane, tells a story in his introduction to volume 2 of Crane's *Work*—some thirty years after the event—of their having walked together on the Bowery one night when Crane, approached by a streetwalker, "placed his left hand upon his heart, removed his hat, and made a most gallant bow . . . [an] exquisite gesture of chivalry." To her query, "Can you show me anything?" Crane replied, "Yes, I can show you the way out, but if you prefer to remain—." As Berryman remarks, "the way out" in *Maggie* is death; but death is not the only way.

"If it were necessary to avow a marriage to save a girl who is not a prostitute from being arrested as a prostitute, it must be done, although the man suffer eternally," Crane wrote in a hitherto unreported account of his appearance in a New York police court on behalf of a woman arrested for soliciting. On September 16, 1896, having arranged to write "a series of studies of life in New York" for the *Journal,* Crane spent the day at the court in Jefferson market; but, the editor's introduction to his story continues, "The novelist felt. . . . He must know more of that throng of unfortunates; he must study the police court victims in their haunts." In this quest he spent the evening in "a Broadway resort" with two "chorus girls" and "a woman of the streets," looking for trouble, as it were. The girl whose arrest Crane protested was one Dora Clark, companion of the woman whose husband he had claimed to be. Dora Clark, or, to use her real name, Ruby Young, was being cruelly framed by the police: Crane had been present at the alleged solicitation, and knew it to be a lie. Little else though he knew about "Dora Clark," he must take the stand in her behalf. Crane wrote down his reasons scrupulously for the newspaper public: were he bound to discretion by such hostages as a job with a business firm, or a wife, or a titled fiancée, he might not have the courage to go through with her defense. But none of these possibly extenuating circumstances at present protects him from his own conscience, and so he must become "a reluctant laggard witness."

His first act, then, in defense of the two women was to pretend to be married to one of them— "it must be done, although the man suffer eternally." For his temerity, in testifying in her defense, the New York police force hounded Crane out of the city. He never lived in New York again.

A few years later there is another woman in Crane's life whose status as a prostitute is not even as equivocal as that of Dora Clark or her friend. Once again, he pretended to marry her.

> Thou art my love,
> And thou art the ashes of other men's love,
> And I bury my face in these ashes,
> And I love them—
> Woe is me.
>
> ("Intrigue" 1)

Crane seems in this poem, as in the earlier news story, masochistically to invite suffering. Yet his life with Cora Howarth, Taylor Stewart Crane, later McNeill, brought him as close to happiness as he ever came. As though to oblige the Crane biographer's desire for a symbolic nexus of his psychic compulsions, Cora, who actually did marry two husbands before Crane and one more after his death, never solemnized her vows, as the saying goes, with the one man who made her happy. The poems in "Intrigue," however, anticipate no satisfactions; the mood is defeated, the tone nostalgic and sentimental. "In loving me once / Thou gave me an eternal privilege / For I can think of thee," the final poem concludes. Through most of "Intrigue" one must agree with Thomas Beer that "his erotic verse drops into the banal." It is indeed surprising to find such a clutter of "thee's" and "thou's," such absurdly sentimental outbursts as "I weep and I gnash, / And I love the little shoe, / The little, little shoe," coming so late in his career—after *The Black Riders* and at least half of the poems in *War Is Kind*. Amy Lowell concluded that Crane "is losing his grip . . . poetry is sliding from him . . . it had been no more with him than a breath of adolescence."

> I thought of the thunder that lived in my head,
> And I wished to be an ogre,
> And hale and haul my beloved to a castle,
> And there use the happy cruel one cruelly,
> And make her mourn with my mourning.

Unlike most of the poem, these lines succeed in finding images that dramatize the violent emotions felt; elsewhere the tone is soliloquy or self-pitying rumination. Yet the sado-masochism of this successful passage suggests that the whole of "Intrigue" may be of more interest to the investigator of Crane's psyche than to the analyst of his poetic achievement.

Let us for a moment pursue the psychological inquiry—or rather, follow Mr. Berryman while he pursues it. Perhaps to assume that Crane "seems to address" Cora in these poems where "love is a doom" is to oversimplify somewhat a psychological condition baffling in its complexity. Berryman, whose assumption on this particular point I question, demonstrates elsewhere the compulsive repetition of circumstances in which Crane became involved—or deliberately involved himself—with women. For reasons which will in a moment become clear, I think "Intrigue" refers only incidentally to Cora.

Berryman's theory is this: he proposes that Crane fulfills with exactitude the four "conditions of love" described by Freud in his study of "A Special Type of Choice of Objects Made by Men" (1910). The first condition, Freud observes, is "the need for an injured third party," that is to say the woman desired can be "only one in regard to whom another man has some right of possession, whether as husband, betrothed, or near friend." She must in the second place be "more or less sexually discredited"; her "fidelity and loyalty" must be open to "some doubt." This condition may be met "within a significant series" ranging from a flirtatious married woman to an actual prostitute. Third, "a high degree of compulsion . . . sincerity and intensity" characterize the lover, whose "passionate attachments of this kind are frequently repeated many times . . . each an exact replica of the others." External circumstances, "such as changes of residence and environment," may lead "to a long chain of such experiences." And finally, "The trait in this type of lover that is most astonishing to the observer is the desire they express to 'rescue' the beloved."

What is one to make of this disturbing constellation? These peculiar conditions of choice, Freud avers, "have the same source as the normal attitude in love." Being derived from "a fixation of the infantile forms of tenderness for the mother," they "represent one of the forms in which this fixation expresses itself." It is evident, Freud says, that the injured third party "is none other than the father himself." The second condition—sexual debasement of the woman—is said to result from the child's discovery of his parents' sexual relations and his consequent "cynical" identification of mother and harlot. "In the light of this new knowledge he begins to desire the mother herself and to hate the father anew for standing in his way; he comes, as we say, under the sway of the Oedipus complex." The compulsive repetition is explained because "the pressing desire in the unconscious for some irreplaceable thing often resolves itself into an endless series . . . [since] the satisfaction longed for is . . . never found in any surrogate."

The significance of the rescue element is more complex. Freud takes this to be "an exceptionally felicitous 'rationalization' of an unconscious motive":

> rescuing the mother acquires the significance of giving her a child or making one for her—one like himself, of course. The departure from the original meaning of the idea of "saving life" is not too great. . . . The mother gave him his own life and. . . . The son shows his gratitude by wishing to have a son by his mother

that shall be like himself; in this rescue fantasy, that is, he identifies himself completely with the father. All the instincts, the living, the grateful, the sensual, the defiant, the self-assertive and
independent—all are gratified in the wish to be *the father of
himself*. Even the element of danger is not lost in the change of
meaning; the experience of birth itself . . . is in fact the first of
all dangers to life, as well as the prototype of all the later ones
we fear.

If this last intricate tangle of displaced identities and masked wish-
fulfillments is at all present in Crane's work it surely remains latent, not
manifest. Yet when Berryman has adduced Crane's attachment for, and wish
to rescue—from plights sometimes imaginary—the betrothed Helen Trent
(1891); Mrs. Lily Brandon Munroe (1894); the street girl reported by Davis,
Mrs. Dora Watts Bowen, Dora Clark and her chorus girl friend, and a widowed
actress named Amy Leslie (all in 1896), as well as Cora, whom he met late
in that year, the probability is strong that the biographer is right in propos-
ing Freud's essay as a "description and explanation of reality" with respect
to Crane's psychic makeup. Newly recovered writings by Crane in the
Columbia University collection, as well as the readings I offer in the present
chapter of his love poems, further incline me to feel that this is the likely case.
Such conclusions can at best be only tentative, however, and it should be stated
that my only concern with this psychological theory is to take whatever help
may be available from it in the interpretation, first, of the poems of Crane's
that are now before us, and second, of the sensibility which created them.
The value of the Freudian theory is probably greater to Crane's biographer
than to the critic of his verse; still, it would seem to explain certain recurrent
patterns in both his actions and the images of his writings; it makes possible
likely inferences as to the areas of experience most available to his imagination; and it suggests the probable limits on some important choices of the
materials and metaphors of his art. All this is merely inferential, however;
even tentative conclusions must be wrung from the writings themselves.
    Helpful as it may be, it is nonetheless inadvisable to rely exclusively on
such a psychological approach, for its inherent emphasis upon the configura-
tions of the individual psyche tends to isolate the investigation of an author's
work from the cultural currents in terms of which his assumptions about life
are also strongly conditioned. Brilliant as are his conjectural linkages of Crane's
images, Mr. Berryman seems to me to be in some measure culpable in this
respect. His study takes little account of a possibility raised by my previous
chapter, namely, that Crane's mode of interpreting experience was deeply

influenced by the religious doctrines which comprise the chief furniture of his cultural heritage. This I think to be true with respect to his poems on love. To the extent that emotion and metaphor from Crane's religious background control his work, it may be advisable to modify somewhat Berryman's predominantly Freudian interpretation of his writings.

Crane's love poems deal in greater particularity than does his fiction with the situations and feelings his "special type of choice of objects" imposed upon him. They are thus crucially revelatory of an important part of his sensibility, despite the fact that on the whole the imaginative world of his verse is a narrower one than that presented in his stories; in a later chapter we shall try to find the reasons for this limitation. The principal images of Crane's love poetry do not for the most part correspond to the governing metaphors of his prose. It would seem that he reserved certain phases of his experience for poetic treatment, and to deal with them he developed a cluster of imagery to some extent independent of that in the rest of his work.

Crane's main body of fictional metaphors has been elucidated by Mr. Berryman's Freudian exploration in the concluding chapter of his book. There he asserts that what is usually taken to be fear in Crane's work is actually "something else . . . the possibility of fatal intervention," which he characterizes as panic. Conjecturally, he traces this panic back to the primal situations for which all later expressions of panic in Crane are unconscious displacements. There are two such hypothesized situations: when twelve years old, Crane, riding his pony, had seen a white girl being stabbed by her Negro lover in the woods; and when he was very young—less than four—he had nightmares of black riders rising from the surf, a dream associated with a still earlier experience of being made by his mother to ride a white horse of which he was terrified. The violence of the stabbing, Berryman suggests, is later generalized under the aspect of war, while its erotic context is preserved in recurrent images of Negroes, knives, or razors, which are further linked to Crane's father shaving and to barbers; a conjectured Swedish barber in Crane's hometown supplies a link to Swedes, Dutchmen, and Germans in his work, and the explanation for the name of Henry Fleming in *The Red Badge* and for the nationality of the ineluctable victim in "The Blue Hotel." The Civil War obsesses Crane, Berryman suggests, because it was "precisely *about the Negro.*" But the Oedipal situation is a familial civil war in which aggression is directed against surrogates for the father, who are characterized by tenor voices, chieftainship, or priestly rank. Aggression is also incipient in the striking namelessness of Crane's characters, a denial of patronym as well as a masking of identity. Berryman emphasizes Crane's alleged feelings of desertion following his father's early death. The chief image of aggression in Crane's work in the horse.

Images in the love poems are not as elaborately disguised or as intricately linked as the foregoing, nor are they drawn from so varied a range of experiences and associations. Love is characteristically associated with longing, despair, and violence, the latter sometimes manifested in metaphors of war or predation. The woman loved may be represented in synecdoche by her white arms, a maternal image which, when linked to erotic contexts, is accompanied by metaphors of cosmic catastrophe. She may be shown as sexually promiscuous, a feared aggressor; in this connection occur snakes, desert, sin, and punishment. Further associations are loyalty and desertion, courage and cowardice. Ever recurrent is the rescue theme, sometimes in contexts involving war and horses.

The poetic effectiveness of these images we shall shortly examine, but we must first return to Stephen Crane's amatory adventures. . . .

Crane's attitude toward war is anything but passive, and we have seen how curiously the imagining of war intrudes upon the mood of his defeat in love in "Flagons of despair." Crane's most ambitious love poem is his largest failure. In some other poems, however, if the suffering was passive its objectification in verse invests it with energy sufficient to give the illusion, essential to art, that the poetic statement controls as well as describes the experience it evokes in the beholder.

We may take, for example, a poem (WK 6; the abbreviations BR and WK will refer to *The Black Riders* and *War Is Kind,* respectively. Unless otherwise specified, the edition used is *The Collected Poems of Stephen Crane,* edited by Wilson Follett [New York, 1930].) whose meaning is similar to that of much of "Intrigue." Developing the theme of brevity in his note to Cora, quoted above, the poem tells us that love is momentary; Crane likens it to "the passing of a ship at night." This is one of his best pieces—Berryman quotes it to illustrate his observation that in *War Is Kind* "There swelled . . . if anyone had listened—a strange singing." But before quoting it here I wish to trace the stages in its development. We know so little about the way Crane's imagination worked, so little about what it selected from the improbable events of his life to work on, that an interest attaches to the derivation of those poems whose starting places we can trace.

The unlikely point of departure for poem 6 is this entry in Cora's manuscript book, on the page following her thoughts about the hopelessness of expecting "uninterrupted reaches of happiness":

Ships that pass in the night and speed each other in passing

> Only a signal shown, and a distant voice in the darkness,
> So, on the ocean of life, we pass and speak one another
> Only a look and a voice, then darkness again and a silence.

Cora, whose commonplace book includes excerpts from Byron, Shakespeare, Burns, Keats, Mrs. Browning, *David Copperfield,* Seneca, George Eliot, and the doggerel of one Philander Johnson, knew also these lines from Longfellow's *Tales of a Wayside Inn.* She must have recited them to Crane; for why else would Longfellow's images be transfigured in this note of his to her?

> Love comes like the tall swift shadow of a ship at night. There
> is for a moment, the music of the water's turmoil, a bell, perhaps,
> a man's shout, a row of gleaming yellow lights. Then the slow sink-
> ing of this mystic shape. Then silence and a bitter silence—the
> silence of the sea at night.
>
> Stephen Crane

We can surmise from Crane's little parody of "The Psalm of Life" that Longfellow was hardly his favorite poet. Why should the abstract "Ships that pass in the night" have released in Crane's imagination these vivid concretions, this strange intensification of mood? Perhaps because certain links in Longfellow's passage were already present in Crane's mind. The conjunction of *boat*: *signal light*: *shout*: *darkness*: *silence* (with darkness already intensified to something more menacing) turns up, with the elements in almost exactly this order, in the manuscript of a press dispatch, apparently never printed. This was written in the spring of 1895 while Crane was in Mexico City. He is describing a nocturnal boat ride on the Viga Canal:

> The musicians played slumberously. We did not wish to hear any
> too well. It was better to lie and watch the large stars come out
> and let the music be merely a tale of the past, a recital from the
> possessions of one's memory, an invoking of other songs, other
> nights. For, after all, the important part of these dreamful times
> to the wanderer is that they cry to him with emotional and tender
> voices of his past. The yellow glitter of the lantern at the boat-
> man's feet made his shadow to be a black awful thing that hung
> angrily over us. There was a sudden shrill yell from the darkness.
> There had almost been a collision. In the blue velvet of the sky,
> the stars had gathered in thousands.

Some of the sentimentality of "Intrigue" is suggested by the yearnings here, but the threatening images of boatman and collision point ahead to other writings more powerful. From this manuscript comes the key that locked Longfellow's lines into Crane's imagination: the context of unfulfilled love in association with the images of ship, signal, voice, darkness. And for Crane, love never comes without menace.

It is a temptation to make of his note to Cora a Crane poem, so close are the rhythms of its phrases to those of his "lines." Crane himself soon wrote a poem using this chain of images, but he was to speak quite a different language, and to establish more dramatically a point of view from which the action is recorded. These lines first appeared in the *Bookman* for October 1896:

> I explain the silvered passing of a ship at night,
> The sweep of each sad lost wave
> The dwindling of the steel thing's striving,
> The little cry of a man to a man,
> A shadow falling across the greyer night,
> And the sinking of the small star;
> Then the waste, the far waste of waters,
> And the soft lashing of black waves
> For long and in loneliness.
>
> Remember thou, O ship of love,
> Thou leavest a far waste of waters,
> And the soft lashing of black waves
> For long and in loneliness.
>
> (WK 6)

Now the motion of the ship is fully realized in "sweep," "dwindling," the falling shadow and sinking star. Longfellow's vague "distant voice" had in Crane's note become "a man's shout," and in the Mexican article, "a sudden shrill yell," but the final "little cry of a man to a man" best expresses the poignant attempt to break through the silence of isolation to another soul. A manuscript of this poem at Columbia has "Oh, thou, my ship in thy stern straight journey" instead of "Remember, thou, O ship of love." Although the latter suggests perhaps too closely the didacticism of Longfellow ("Sail on, O Ship of State") or Holmes, the poem must somewhere specify what it is all about. Yet once we know that, the rejected alternative is revealing too: love travels a "stern straight journey"; why this must be so to Crane we shall shortly see. More intrinsic to the present poem is the success with which a set of associated concepts has been rendered in concrete objective images, the very rhythms and sounds of which contribute in the reader's imagination to both the action and the emotion the poet wishes to create there.

"You have the most beautiful arms I ever saw," Crane wrote to Helen Trent in 1891. "If I could keep your arms nothing else would count. It would not matter if there was nothing else to hope for in the world or if there was no more world. In dreams, don't you ever fall and fall but not be afraid of anything because somebody safe is with you?" But the next day the twenty-year-old lover was stunned to learn that Miss Trent would soon be married in London. Nine years later, Beer remarks with felicitous irony, "when an Englishman pointed out the celebrated Stephen Crane, she saw him across the flare of a London theatre without knowing why he was celebrated. But in 'The Black Riders,' on the eleventh page":

> Should the wide world roll away,
> Leaving black terror,
> Limitless night,
> Nor God, nor man, nor place to stand
> Would be to me essential,
> If thou and thy white arms were there,
> And the fall to doom a long way.
>
> (BR 10)

In this earliest love poem, love is already a desolation. These seven lines give us several attitudes and images typical of Crane's verse on this subject. "Black terror" reminds us of "the terrible heedless courage of babes" —we find courage and terror continually invoked in contexts of love. Another strange thing: to symbolize the woman's beauty and erotic attraction Crane mentions, of all her parts and qualities, only "thy white arms." Her arms will prove to be a repeated image whose other appearances bear examination. Finally, although her arms would save him from "the fall to doom," what the poem really says is that he is doomed and fallen because he loves her. Surely this is one of the most joyless love poems ever written. Crane's attitude is paradox, the antithesis of romance; his ambivalence is partly due to the grim grasp upon his imagination of Bishop Peck's damnatory doctrines. Crane's natural impulse is deeply, wildly romantic, but he is inhibited by that "swift hand" from the sky which he hates but has not yet fended away. Thus "Black terror, / Limitless night" are his expected portion.

To begin with, why does Crane mention only her arms? We find in "Intrigue" too the loved one's arms are prominent as a symbol of her erotic spell (3, 6, 10) and of his passive suffering (3). There are occasional references to lips, face, voice, but none so recurrent as these. Crane's love poems are strangely barren of descriptions of the beloved. What is unusual here is the concentration in *arms*, a maternal image, of significations so intensely erotic. Freud, describing the Oedipal situation, remarks that "the libido has dwelt so long in its attachment to the mother, even after puberty, that the maternal characteristics remain stamped on the love-objects chosen later—so long that they all become easily recognizable as mother-surrogates." Berryman goes on to equate, for Crane, harlot with mother-image. Here it is enough to note that when the arms appear in the poems erotically, the image invokes menacing associations (writhing, frenzy); but when, as in "Should the wide world roll away" and in another poem deferred for later discussion (BR 67), the arms are protective, the emotional context is infinitely more tender. But in the identification of the beloved's arms with protectiveness (a maternal function), the imagined action becomes fearsomely self-destructive: in the first instance, God, man, and the world are rolled away; the second begins, "God lay dead in heaven," and ends with "the jaws of the final beast."

Since to love is to be damned, the meditated action in Crane's poems on love takes place in a *paysage moralisé*. In one of them he writes, "I looked here; / I looked there; / Nowhere could I see my love." But at last he finds her: "She was in my heart" (BR 8). After his meal of a heart in the desert (BR 3), the repetition of "in my heart" sounds ominous. A later poem is more explicit:

> Love walked alone.
> The rocks cut her tender feet,
> And the brambles tore her fair limbs.
>   (BR 41)

This is followed by "I walked in the desert" (42), which remains a desert to him although "A voice said, 'It is no desert.'" We remember what the heart-eater was eating: "From within, out of the heart of men, proceed evil thoughts, adulteries, fornications . . . laciviousness." Since love, sexual love, is the epitome of all sin, such paradises as the romantic aspires to must be abjured:

> Places among the stars,
> Soft gardens near the sun,
> Keep your distant beauty;
> . . . .
> Since she is here
> In a place of blackness
> Here I stay and wait.
>   (BR 23)

These themes of the waste land, sexual love, and sin are joined again in poem 11 of *War Is Kind*. "On the desert" a tribe "Of hooded men, squat and dumb" watch a woman snake-dancer:

> mystic things, sinuous, dull with terrible colour,
> Sleepily fondle her body
> Or move at her will
> . . . .
> Slow, menacing and submissive.

There is no other action in this erotic tableau. But the last lines recall again the heart-eater relishing his bitter feast:

> The dignity of the accursèd;
> The glory of slavery, despair, death,
> Is the dance of the whispering snakes.

The Arabian houri is an apt image for the type of love we have seen Crane pursue. As the exhibitionistic lover of the many "hooded men" she is sexually discredited. Their hoods may link them with the snakes that fondle her body—cobras no doubt—yet we note that their responsibility for sexual initiative is partly suppressed by the suggestion of sleep, or wholly transferred as the snakes "move at *her* will . . . submissive."

In other poems, too, we find the initiative taken by the woman, who is therefore dangerous. In this context the image of snakes recurs. Linton, hero of "The Squire's Madness," Crane's only story about a "poet," has difficulty completing these lines (not included in *Collected Poems*):

> The garlands of her hair are snakes;
> Black and bitter are her hating eyes.
> A cry the windy death-hall wakes—
> O, love, deliver us.
> The flung cup rolls to her sandal's tip;
> His arm—

> Whereupon his thought fumed over the next two lines, coursing like greyhounds after a fugitive vision of writhing lover, with the foam of poison on his lips, dying at the feet of the woman.

In this tale the wife thinks her absent-minded and distressed poet insane, and persuades him to see a brain specialist. But the diagnosis is: *"It is your Wife who is Mad! Mad as a Hatter!"* Truer than the observed reality of the prose—his distracted air and practical incompetence—were the fears expressed in his poem.

Earlier, in "Intrigue," the same combination appears of woman as feared aggressor, doom, and snake:

> Thou art my love,
> And thou art a priestess,
> And in thy hand is a bloody dagger,
> And my doom comes to me surely—
> Woe is me.
>
> Thou art my love,
> And thou art a skull with ruby eyes,
> And I love thee—
>
> ("Intrigue" 1)

The significance of the usually phallic snake is ambiguous in these poems. We may better understand it after consulting Crane's story, "The Snake" (1896), in which a man and a snake confront each other with "hatred and fear":

> Individuals who do not participate in this strife incur the investigations of scientists. Once there was a man and a snake who were friends, and at the end the man lay dead with the marks of the snake's caress just over his East Indian heart.

One might take the rest of this sketch to be realism, or, perhaps in view of a passage on snakes in hell, a theological parable. But the two sentences just cited point in another direction. Along with hatred and fear of snakes, Crane feels an inescapable fascination—not to know it is to be unnatural, an object of puzzled scientific scrutiny. And the second sentence, itself a fable complete, brings us back to the whispering snakes in the desert: again we are in the Orient, and the snake caresses the lover's heart. Hidden beneath the narrative level of the sketch, contributing to its almost unbearable intensity, is this masked sexual anxiety. It is well to remember how shocked Crane's good father had been at such milder sins as drinking, dicing, and cards; how zealous a Methodist was his mother; how ascetic the ethics of *What Must I Do to Be Saved?* It is likely that Crane approached sex with tremendous inhibitions and guilt. Part of the explanation for his attachment to harlots may have been a conviction that if the "sexually discredited" woman initiates sexual activity, her lover may be partly absolved of the guilt. The snake image in these poems and tales is also to be taken in its theological signification as the agent of man's fall, the inciter to sin. Thus the lover, in the Squire's poem, taking the poisoned cup of sin (a flagon of despair) from his snake-haired Medusa (possibly a mother image), becomes a viper himself, and dies. This fate,

however, is what human nature has in store for us, "The dignity of the ac-
cursèd" which Crane has celebrated in his poem about the heart-eater and
in "A god came to a man" in the Garden of Eden.

STANLEY WERTHEIM

Stephen Crane
and the Wrath of Jehova

Human isolation in its physical, emotional, or ideological manifestations has retained its prominence as the pervasive theme of American literature, and this is undoubtedly because loneliness is an integral factor in American life itself. Our best novels are maturation stories whose central characters—Ishmael, Huckleberry Finn, Isabel Archer—are nonconformists entering upon the currents of experience without formal commitments or the support of creeds. This problem of the relationship of the uninitiated individual to the social and natural universe lies at the heart of Stephen Crane's writings. His autobiographical protagonists are Isolatoes engaged in an unsuccessful struggle to integrate their lives with that of society and yet preserve separate identities.

Crane's youthful revolt from a restrictive fundamentalist religious environment determined the battleground of both his inner conflicts and his view of man as alone in a hostile universe. His maternal grandfather and granduncle, George and Jesse Peck, were prominent Methodist clergymen who had grown into manhood amid the frontier evangelism of western New York in the early nineteenth century. The emotional frenzy of revival Methodism was carried over into Jesse Peck's *What Must I Do to Be Saved?* a hortatory tract redolent with the fumes of sulphur and brimstone. A copy of this book was presented to Jonathan Townley Crane by the author and was left by the elder Crane as a legacy to his son. It was found among Stephen's effects at Brede Place with his childhood inscription still clearly legible. The tract offers ample evidence of the emphasis on natural depravity which Mrs. Crane brought into her marriage. "A mass of loathesome corruption alone," Jesse Peck had insisted, "can show how vile is the depravity of man." Crane described his mother as a single-minded woman who "lived in and for religion" and was

From *Literary Review* 7, no. 4 (Summer 1964). © 1964 by *Literary Review*.

offended by the suggestion that any of her children might be "slipping from Grace and giving up eternal damnation or salvation or those things." She became the prototype of the dogmatic but ineffectual maternal figures of her son's fiction—Mary Johnson, Mrs. Fleming, Mrs. Kelcey—who mouth pious phrases but invariably fail their children at crucial moments.

Crane's biographers have continued to insist that his mother held religious views much more narrow and more condemnatory than those of her husband. Yet there is no reason to believe that serious doctrinal or temperamental differences existed between Jonathan Crane and his wife. The Reverend Dr. Crane was converted from the Presbyterian faith at the age of eighteen, because he could no longer subscribe to the theory of infant damnation. Although he had forsaken Calvinistic determinism and accepted the Arminian position that salvation may be achieved through the faith of the individual, the distinction between the justified and the unregenerate remained sharp in his theology, and he had by no means given up the fiery pit: "He that believeth not is condemned; he that believeth is saved," the elder Crane thundered in *Holiness, the Birthright of All God's Children*. Until the moment that the penitent passes from unbelief to belief his condition is "one of inexpressible evil. He is guilty, condemned, corrupt, helpless, the wrath of God resting on him, and hell waiting his coming, with its eternal darkness and despair."

Jonathan Crane was a puritan of the puritans. His neurotic antipathy for sensual indulgence was embodied in four books which his libertine son retained in his library until his death in 1900. *An Essay on Dancing* (1849), *The Right Way* (1853), *Popular Amusements* (1869), and *Arts of Intoxication* (1870) had a wide circulation among Methodists and were extremely influential. These tracts reveal a narrowly pedantic mind, virtually obsessed with the need to condemn the most innocent amusements as machinations of the Devil. In addition to setting forth the horrible consequences of such dissipations as dancing, drinking, and gambling, they denounce smoking, horse races, circuses, theatres, chess, billiards, baseball, and the reading of novels. Indeed, twice as much space in *Popular Amusements* is devoted to the sinfulness of novel reading than any other of the transgressions dealt with. Particularly objectionable are novels which portray violence or strong emotion. As depraved as the user of alcohol is the individual who permits himself "to revel in nauseous descriptions of lawless passion and bloody deeds."

Clearly, Jonathan Crane was more straight-laced than the average clergyman of his day. Although the Methodist church in America had acquired a reputation for austerity, few of its ministers objected to baseball, chess, or smoking, and the *Christian Advocate* regularly carried advertisements for novels. But Jonathan Crane was a dour disciple of Saint Paul, whose Epistles it was his particular pleasure to quote. The concern with isolation, spiritual impoverishment, and fear in his youngest son's writing was an outgrowth of the guilt concomitant with his defiance of his father's God. He reveled in the vices denounced in Jonathan Crane's books: he smoked incessantly and drank immoderately; his single year of higher education was spent in baseball games and poker sessions; not only did he read novels depicting strong emotions but he wrote them; during his last years in England he had an unusual interest in horseback riding. To a psychology professor who once admonished him for his conduct Crane replied, "I know what Saint Paul says, but I disagree with Saint Paul."

The theme of revolt against the father is exemplified more clearly in the life and work of Stephen Crane than in any other American writer. His clerical forbears had insisted that the heart was loathsome and the source of all evil, and Crane nowhere denied that man was a fallen sinner. Yet, as an artist it was essential for him to express that which was within his heart, although it was bitter, and he preferred to identify with fallen humanity rather than to worship transcendent injustice. The wrathful Jehova who issued from the pens of Jesse Peck and Jonathan Crane created man with desires and then proceeded to condemn him for expressing them. Crane's sense of justice was outraged by this cosmic dilemma. Against the brutal villain of the Old Testament he set an interior God of simple human compassion:

> A man went before a strange god,—
> The god of many men, sadly wise.
> And the diety thundered loudly,
> Fat with rage, and puffing:
> "Kneel, mortal, and cringe
> And grovel and do homage
> To my particularly sublime majesty."
>
> The man fled.
>
> Then the man went to another god,—
> The god of his inner thoughts.
> And this one looked at him
> With soft eyes
> Lit with infinite comprehension,
> And said: "My poor child!"

This inner voice of mercy takes men out of the Christian churches where ministers threaten in the name of a menacing Jehova. It allows them to recognize their brotherhood in sin. However, it is not a shield against the indifference or hostility of the natural and social universe. For the Peck family and for Jonathan Crane, the God of Wrath was a mighty fortress, a bulwark against the black riders of sin, but a vague bond of sympathy offered inadequate protection. Guilt, anxiety, and psychic isolation were the penalties which Crane paid for his defiance. "You must go alone before the bar of God," Jesse Peck had warned. "You must answer for your own life of guilt, and you yourself must, if finally impenitent, obey the terrific words, 'Depart ye cursed, into everlasting fire.' You alone must suffer for your obstinate rebellion." Crane cut himself off from the ancestral ties which threatened his independence and stifled his aspirations as a writer but which had been the original basis of his childhood security. His rejection of the firm moral code embodied in the manuals of piety compiled by his father was essential, but it left him with a feeling of isolation in a hostile universe which found expression in all his writings and culminated in the desperate soul searching of *The Red Badge of Courage.*

Crane, therefore, with his personal sense of alienation from his ethical and religious roots as well as from the materialistic, self-assertive spirit of his generation was peculiarly well-equipped to become the analyst of the terrified soul. The "eels of despair" which lay wet and cold against the back of the New York Kid in the story of "The Five White Mice," the quaking apprehension of the wild-eyed Collins of "A Mystery of Heroism," "mad from the threats of destruction," and Henry Fleming's anxieties about his courage were familiar states of mind to the minister's son from New Jersey whose emotional life was dominated by fear and loneliness.

Physical, social, and spiritual isolation in the face of danger and possible death became the characteristic emotional state of Crane's protagonists. This is evident in his earliest works of fiction, the Sullivan County sketches, which are focused upon the exploits of an anonymous "little man" who is separated from his companions and placed in perilous situations to which he reacts with terror and impotent rage. In Crane's more mature work the individual is usually rebuffed when he attempts to achieve social integration. Dr. Trescott of "The Monster" is baffled when he finds himself ostracized for a charitable act in a community which professes a Christian view of human affairs. The lieutenant in "An Episode of War" discovers that his wounded arm is an unwelcome reminder of mortality to his comrades and estranges them from him, and the correspondent of "The Open Boat" learns that despite "the subtle brotherhood of men" established upon the sea, each man must make his way to shore alone when the moment of crisis comes.

The opening tableau of *Maggie* reveals the pattern of counterpointed struggle and indifference which typifies Crane's central theme of the isolation of the individual in a hostile or unconcerned universe. The little boy standing upon a heap of gravel "for the honor of Rum Alley" is confronted by a ring of juvenile assailants who encircle him in the instinctive manner of the wolf pack. Juxtaposed to this turbulent scene is a group of callous onlookers, epitomizing the moral apathy of a society familiar with violence and inured to human suffering. Indifference is what betrays Maggie. The true villains of her melodrama are social institutions—the tenement, the sweatshop, the saloon, and particularly the church. Crane made the most of the opportunity which this study of the slums gave him to attack the institution to which his father's life had been dedicated. The heartlessness of human relationships in this world peopled by characters whose names are ironic mockeries of central figures in the New Testament—Mary, Peter, Thomas, James—is unrelieved by the blatant self-righteousness of mission evangelism. Particularly virulent is Crane's depiction of Christian ministers—harsh, narrow men, so obsessed with their condemnatory theology that they are able to give to the worn people who come to their missions from the world of strife and poverty only a further promise of condemnation.

After they had left the mission where the preacher had threatened " 'You are damned' " and the souls of the people had replied " 'Where's our soup?' " Jimmie and his companion "confused the speaker with Christ." This is, of course, the point of Crane's satire. The church had betrayed the purpose of Christ's sacrifice by substituting threats of punishment for His redeeming love. The scene has its parallels in *George's Mother* where the mission sermon that Kelcey hears only proves to him that he is damned and in the episode in *The Red Badge of Courage* where Henry Fleming seeks refuge in a forest chapel, only to find a decaying corpse enthroned in the "religious half light." For Maggie total destruction is assured when, after her rejection by Pete, she seeks "the grace of God" and approaches a minister benevolent in appearance. "But as the girl timidly accosted him he made a convulsive movement and saved his respectability by a vigorous sidestep. He did not risk it to save a soul." The novel ends with a grotesque parody of pious sentiment. Maggie's home is ironically transposed into a church, and there is a mock Pietà as Mary Johnson laments the death of her child. Her self-pitying scream, " 'Oh, yes, I'll fergive her! I'll fergive her!' " is a masterful ironic inversion, since in this case it would obviously be more appropriate if the sinner forgave the church.

For Stephen Crane, however, there was no possibility of reconciliation with the church. After the death of his mother he never again entered a place where the avenging God was worshiped, and he self-consciously redoubled his dissipations in the vices that his father had written about or had preached against. When interviewed or when writing a letter which he suspected would be published, he pictured Jonathan Crane as simple and kind, but in his writings he execrated both the man and his doctrines. Even if the heaven of the orthodox existed, Crane would not allow his father to share in its rewards:

> Walking in the sky,
> A man in strange black garb
> Encountered a radiant form.
> Then his steps were eager;
> Bowed he devoutly.
> "My Lord," said he.
> But the spirit knew him not.

Despite his rejection of repressive orthodoxy Crane could not rid himself of the dilemma of religious conscience. His mind was ruled by the dread of punishment, and, therefore, in all his work he portrayed the individual as isolated in a universe of primal forces which ignore or threaten his existence. When *The Red Badge of Courage* was published, many of the reviewers took it for granted that Crane had personally experienced battle, and in a figurative sense this assumption was correct. Although he had never seen warfare or been in physical danger of any form, Crane was thoroughly familiar with the anatomy of fear. Into his parable of the Civil War he projected the same religious conflicts found in *The Black Riders*. The sinful boy who had rebelled against the Unjust Father and in so doing had separated himself from the community of the faithful became the youth who in panic fled from the protection of the tribe and who was, therefore, forced to wander in a fearful hinterland in order to redefine his identity and to learn his relationship to nature and to society.

The Red Badge of Courage is an aborted initiation myth into which Crane projected his own failure to find internal security within social conventions. The protagonist is an untried youth, separated from the warm fantasies of childhood and brought to the threshold of life symbolized by a world at war. The tests he must pass are those of endurance in battle and loyalty to comrades, and the reward is tribal acceptance. The supreme ordeal consists, of course, in the ability to face unflinchingly the death-dealing fire of the enemy. The hero of the mythological initiation journey is often given a guide or helper who escorts the adventurer to the place of conflict and sometimes provides him with weapons against the dragon forces he is about to meet. In classical myth such figures are represented by Hermes-Mercury, Charon, or the Sybil who directs the descent of Aeneas into Avernus. In Christian story this is the function of the Holy Ghost. For Henry Fleming, as for Stephen Crane himself, the embodiment of the Christian spirit in the Bible was inadequate as an aid in resolving the variegations of the soul, and thus Crane expunged from the published novel and manuscript passages in which Henry's mother gave him a Bible as a guide in the spiritual wilderness.

Not only do creeds fail to explain the purpose of existence, but the experience of comrades proves equally fruitless. Henry discovers that his companions are without emotional awareness or even the need to develop insight. Jim Conklin and Wilson, the loud soldier, typify the common run of humanity. Conklin represents the phlegmatic man who docilely accepts cosmic anarchy and falls as an accidental victim of the war god, while Wilson is an aggressive blusterer whose unintelligent and ineffectual resistance finally ends in conformity. The man with the cheery voice who leads Henry back to his regiment after he has received his dishonorable wound from the rifle butt of a panicked Union soldier functions as an almost supernatural guide in the wilderness. Henry's conductor is, however, no enlightened saint or prophet but also a wanderer, " 'hollerin' here an' hollerin' there, in th' damn' darkness.' " Like Jim Conklin, he is an unreflective individual, but where Conklin is passive and fatalistic, the man with the cheery voice is a creature of strong conviction. His watchword is faith— " 'It's goin' t' be long huntin'. But I guess we kin do it.' " Yet he is emotionally and intellectually unconcerned with the problem of salvation. Amid the confused fighting of the day, he admits to the youth, " 'I couldn't tell t' save m' soul which side I was on.' " To a mind such as his, capable of blind credence, assurance is unnecessary. For Henry Fleming, the victim of a disjointed, isolated psyche, such confidence in the future is impossible, and this is perhaps why he cannot recognize his helper. "As he who had so befriended him was thus passing out of his life, it suddenly occurred to the youth that he had not once seen his face." Faith can bring Henry within sight of the campfires of his regiment, up to the threshold of salvation, but cannot accompany him across it, and he finds himself in the position of a hopelessly deracinated individual.

To be sure, the youth fights bravely on the second day of battle. His doubts and fears seem to dissolve, and he immerses himself completely in the business of war. This is not because Henry has suddenly attained maturity, as so many critics of *The Red Badge* have insisted, but because he transfers to the enemy the animal fury he had previously directed against the cosmic scheme. "Yesterday, when he had imagined the universe to be against him, he had hated it, little gods and big gods; today he hated the army of the foe with the same great hatred." The culminating dramatic irony of the novel, therefore, is in the paradoxical resolution of the hero quest. Henry earns recognition and a tenuous place in the social order, but he does so not by consciously accepting the values of the group but by debasing his human qualities in order to act as an animal in battle. In terms of a change in character—in the sense that this means the transformation of moral resolutions into actions—the youth makes little if any progress. He has attained neither spiritual salvation nor true maturity and has gained only a partial victory over the monsters of fear and self doubt. What he has learned is that human behavior is largely determined by emotional reactions to environmental conditions and not by heroic ideals. Crane brought his protagonist up to the threshold of maturity but would not allow him to cross it, for he did not believe that true maturity, which involves a structured relationship between an individual and his environment, was ever possible in a universe of irrational and unpredictable forces.

Crane's loss of faith in religious orthodoxy and traditional ethical values occurred at an early age, and his rejection of the angry Jehova precipitated strong feelings of uncertainty and guilt. Because of this there is an oppressive repetitiveness in the themes of futility, self-deception, and isolation which permeate his writings. Lost in a world which appeared to be a maze without a plan, he submerged himself in nihilism, viewing with chilling objectivity the barren schemes of men who seek to impose patterns of order upon an arbitrary universe. Individuals remain estranged from one another since there are no absolutes, and men cannot coordinate their egocentric desires in a meaningful social community. In the end, Crane stressed personal awareness and self-reliance—the ability to observe the absurd chaos of life unflinchingly, fearing neither the wrath of God nor the judgment of man:

> "Think as I think," said a man,
> "Or you are abominably wicked;
> You are a toad."
>
> And after I had thought of it,
> I said: "I will, then, be a toad."

DANIEL WEISS

"The Blue Hotel"

Even beyond *The Red Badge of Courage* and the other studies of violence, "The Blue Hotel" is, as an intensive study of fear, the finest thing Crane created. It has been compared to Hemingway's "The Killers," which is interesting, since psychologically they are diametrical opposites meeting only at the antipodes— fear itself, for Ole Andreson in "The Killers" exemplifies in almost pathological terms the flight to passivity in his fatalistic resignation to death, and the Swede is the other side of the coin, a pathological flight to activity.

The one weakness of "The Blue Hotel" is perhaps its rational framework. The widespread assumption on the part of easterners and Europeans in the 1890s that the western United States were inhabited solely by cowpokes, Indians, and bandits is used by Crane as a foundation for the Swede's immediate suspicion of everyone. But the Swede is, like Bartleby the Scrivener, an "Isolato," the very mask of fear, and not to be measured by normal standards.

The Swede arrives, with some other travelers, at the Palace Hotel, Nebraska, convinced from the start that he will be robbed and murdered by the proprietor, Pat Scully, his son, Johnnie, or one of the cowboy transients about the place. At first he is timidly apprehensive, then hysterically frightened. Scully calms him down and invites him to play a friendly game of cards with the group. The Swede now undergoes a complete change of personality. He plays cards with manic verve, "board-whacking" as he takes his tricks. The card game is upset when he accuses the proprietor's son Johnnie of cheating, and then beats him in a fist fight. Flushed with this triumph, he extends his circle to the local saloon where, trying to browbeat the local gambler into drinking with him, he meets the death he has long feared.

From *The Critic Agonistes: Psychology, Myth and the Art of Fiction,* edited by Eric Solomon and Stephen Arkin. © 1985 by the University of Washington Press.

The easterner speaks the epilogue. Johnnie, he says, *was* cheating: "And you—you were simply puffing around the place and wanting to fight. And then old Scully himself! We are all in it! . . . Every sin is the result of collaboration. We, five of us, have collaborated in the murder of this Swede."

In considering "The Blue Hotel" in its psychological apposition to *The Red Badge of Courage,* we face first of all an archaeological problem. Excavating for the characterological sources of Henry Fleming's actions, we have run across a structure that is obliquely but intrinsically a part of the counterphobic techniques examined previously in the novel. Digging for the battlefield of Homeric Troy, we have found a city below the ancient site.

The Red Badge of Courage presented a reasonably normal youth making a tolerable adjustment to an unreasonably tough situation. His anxieties were finally and convincingly assuaged when certain psychic imperatives found satisfaction under the shelter of the flag. Certain shadowy relationships, parental and sibling, resolved themselves in the process, with nothing more untoward in their nature than would be compatible with the ambivalences of adolescence—identifications and projections and flights, all in the service of an urgent adjustment to danger.

In "The Blue Hotel" the firm ligature of counterphobic defense technics unites the story with the others that have been considered, but now they are in the service, not of a real danger situation, but of a paranoid delusional system, and all that such a system implies. *The Red Badge of Courage* can be called a strategic fantasy of fear overcome. "The Blue Hotel" is a nightmare.

In discussing *The Red Badge of Courage,* I touched upon Henry Fleming's attempts, first and last, to still his excitement by seeing the war first as the above-mentioned "blue demonstration" and finally as a "matched game." As a defense against a danger situation, either one's own rebellious impulses or an environmental threat, the game satisfies the compulsion to repeat in a mitigated, controlled form an experience which was originally terrifying. Children's games often play out deaths, murders, and mutilations, with the child playing the active role in a drama which originally cast him as its passive, frightened victim. Such games, as we all know, are played with a frantic joy that comes close to being pain. It is, in fact, a joy that celebrates a release from painful anxieties.

There is, in the stories we have considered, a sort of "game syndrome" that operates in this way. We have seen it in the imagery of the novel. It shows itself briefly in "The Price of the Harness," in Nolan's relegating the charge he is involved in to a level of "dream-scenes." In "The Five White Mice" the game is more ambitiously employed; it is an analogous foreshadowing of the main action. The New York Kid in a friendly dice game in the Mexican bar puts fifty dollars, sight unseen, on a die. There are no takers; the die is a low number; he would have lost. The incident passes off in good-natured teasing.

The same bluff and backing down take place in the street, in what the Kid thinks of as the "unreal real." This time the Kid himself is the losing die, and the Spanish grandee is the timid bettor who will not call the Kid's bluff. The full psychological function of the game as a release from anxiety is subordinated to its value as a symbolic statement of self-evaluation. The Kid says, in effect, "I am not what I seem to be, but only my father will call my bluff."

In "The Blue Hotel" the play's the thing, and Crane apparently knew it, the same way he knew something about the inner workings of the Swede somewhere between conscious and intuitive grasp. As a man the Swede is past redemption; the game of cards is not his undoing. It merely serves as the last scrap of reality on which the Swede can found his delusions of persecution.

When the Swede enters the hotel, Scully's son Johnnie and an old farmer are playing cards for fun. Serious money-gambling is too close to reality for mock hostility to function as it does in child's play. Playing for fun, Johnnie and the old man are engaged in serious quarrels over their game. Following each such quarrel the Swede laughs nervously and makes some remark about the dangers of western life, incomprehensible to the others. When he is first invited into the game, he plays nervously and quietly, while the cowboy is the "board-whacker." "A game with a board-whacker in it is sure to become intense," and for the Swede the intensity, because all occasions inform against him, becomes unendurable, and he voices his fears: "I suppose I am going to be killed before I can leave this house."

Old Scully, with a fine sense of the problem, exhibits the domesticity of his life to the Swede, shows pictures of his wife and dead daughter, gives an account of his sons and the life of the town. He draws the Swede into the circle of fraternal fellowship to which his son, the cowboy, and the transients of the Palace Hotel belong. The Swede, finally induced to take a drink (which he first rejects, as Scully says, because he "thought I was tryin' to poison 'im"), discharges all the energy that was part of his anxiety in an outburst of false relief. He becomes a part of the family with a vengeance, presiding over the supper table with a joyless, feverish joy: "The Swede domineered the whole feast and he gave it the appearance of a cruel bacchanal. He seemed to have grown suddenly taller; he gazed, brutally disdainful, into every face. His voice rang through the room."

When he played cards again with the group, he becomes the "board-whacker," while the cowboy is reduced to a sad silence. It is the discovery of Johnnie's cheating that precipitates the tragic sequel. The Swede is mad; he "fizzed like a firewheel"; but the game of cards is a benign way for him to work off his aggressions harmlessly, his hostilities intelligently displaced to the card table. Ironically, however, the game is denied its therapeutic value. The scrap of reality that will nourish the Swede's original delusion, which he has not relinquished, merely mastered, is provided by the fact that Johnnie is *really* cheating. *Real* cheating in a game for fun violates the make-believe, like acid in a water pistol. For the Swede the cheating restores the game to the world of outlaws, professional gamblers, and gunmen. It then follows, with maniacal logic and poetic justice both, that the next and last victim of the Swede's attentions should be the town's professional gambler, whom the Swede unwittingly but unerringly singles out. He is the institutionalized reality of which Johnnie was merely the precursor.

I have reviewed here those elements which relate most apparently to Henry Fleming's actions in *The Red Badge of Courage*. The Swede exhibits, albeit madly, alternate flights to passivity and activity. Wary apprehension succeeds to panic and a passive acceptance of annihilation, to be succeeded by a triumph of mastery, an identification with the aggressor, the pursuer, and no longer the pursued. And above all there is the framework of the game, danger passing off in play, only to return again as danger.

There are other resemblances, however, obscured, not by their existing in "The Blue Hotel" as traces, but because in "The Blue Hotel" these elements are more intense. They have the vividness of mania.

The inference in connection with paranoid delusions of persecution is that the subject is defending himself against his own homosexuality. In his relations with other men he denies his love by substituting an equally dynamic attraction—that of hate. He then denies the hate itself, since it lacks any foundation in reality, and puts upon him moreover the guilty burden of aggression, and projects his hatred upon the object of his original desire. The ego in such cases regresses from its ability to test reality to the archaic delusional systems, the animistic world of childhood, in which all nature is equally sensate. Thus the wish to be the passive victim of some homosexual violation may express itself in the fear of such violation—which displaces itself to other body openings. The fears arise in connection with being poisoned, invaded by dangerous rays, brainwashed. The paranoid may also identify *with* his persecutor in order actively to do to him what he might otherwise have suffered himself. The transformation of the repressed erotic attraction in favor of an overt sadistic aversion finds its literary expression in such relationships as Prince Hal's and Harry Hotspur's, "I will embrace him with a soldier's arm," or Claggart's persecution of Billy Budd in Melville's story.

The Swede's emotional swing from apprehensive depression to manic elation reflects, internalized, the same battlefield as that on which Henry Fleming fought his fears. The problems of self-esteem, alienation, and reunion with the omnipotent superior present themselves, along with the technics of mastery involved. We can only add, tentatively, in view of the Swede's paranoid delusions, that the Swede's anxieties involve the mastery of his own homosexual aggressions rather than a threat from the external world.

Anyone arriving in a strange town will experience that sense of narcissistic starvation that comes with the feeling that one is a social cipher in the life of the community. The Swede, psychotic to begin with, arrives already prejudiced, in a small western town, bringing with him a massive and insatiable need for reassurance against his own unfathomed wishes.

"We'll git swallowed," says a soldier meekly, just before a charge in *The Red Badge of Courage*. It is perfectly descriptive of the oral level of fixation that prevails in a raging battle. Eat or be eaten. The Swede's repressed oral fixations involve "swallowing" the world in order to be reunited with its omnipotence, the way a hungry child cleaves savagely to the breast that comforts it. But the obverse side of the coin is his manifest fear that the world will just as savagely attack him.

In this spirit he refuses the first drink Scully offers him as if Scully's teeth were at his throat. But Scully's kindness and the drink itself, once the Swede has swallowed it and found it harmless—experiences which would, with a rational man, effect a pleasant reunion with society—return the Swede's impulse to its original uninhibited form. Scully behaves like a father to the Swede. What is more, he offers him the oral satisfactions of a drink. " 'Drink,' said the old man affectionately. . . . The Swede laughed wildly. He grabbed the bottle, put it to his mouth; and as his lips curled absurdly around the opening and his throat worked, he kept his glance, *burning with hatred,* upon the old man's face." The image is the image of a fierce baby, its feeding long overdue, glaring over the nipple at the source of its relief.

The combined gestures are the symbolic fulfillment of a deeply repressed fantasy. Scully has, in effect, "adopted" the Swede, whose exaggerated need for assurance and oral sadistic drives will extend themselves to the absorption of everything and everyone in sight. His foster father, Scully, he swallows at one gulp. A few minutes after he has drunk he is contradicting Scully "in a bullying voice," or has "stalked with the air of an owner into the executive parts of the hotel." He must enter into this cannibalistic relationship with everyone at once. In the card game he takes all the tricks. At supper he almost impales the Easterner's hand as they reach for the same biscuit. His fight with Johnnie is a still more intimate encounter, a sibling struggle for the attentions of the same father, the translation into sadistic (and therefore socially plausible) activity of the Swede's repressed homoerotic drives. There is no clear line here between the various components that move the Swede to action. His mind is a graveyard of decaying realities, baseless fears, disguised desires, and futile strategies.

Manic elation is the literal rendering of the ancient "Whom the gods destroy they first make mad." Its shrill laughter and high spirits and a sense of unlimited power are a celebration of the release of the ego from the bonds of a self-derogatory conscience. Now the ego has become the lord of its own misrule and embarks on defiant pursuit of forbidden pleasures, which here involve the aggressive humiliation of other men. The Swede discharges his new, liberated energies in cards, drinking, and fighting. He has achieved his reunion with omnipotence at the expense of his intellect. He has begun in all self-effacing humility by fearing for his life; he ends bloated with his triumph over his imagined persecutors. He *is* the group. His commanding the gambler to drink with him, the sadistic counterpart to Scully's earlier, kinder command, is his moment of *hubris*. He has become the manic travesty of the father. The gambler knifes him, the knife itself a translation (and therefore socially acceptable, more so, at least than its phallic equivalent) of the Swede's repressed wish for sexual violation, and like an enchantment dispelled, the Swede reverts to his former role of the passive hapless victim of another man.

The Easterner's self-accusatory indictment of all of them as murderers— "every sin is the result of a collaboration" —is too oriental, too transcendental a statement to be confined within a blue hotel or a platitude of social consciousness. It has karmic ramifications, whose psychological equivalents are consistent with that omniscient "Indefinite Cause" which threatens to seal Henry Fleming's doom, that fascinated dread and disbelief with which Crane's characters enter onto the stage as spectators and actors both. In summing up "The Five White Mice" John Berryman writes: "The Kid's faith, in substance—Crane's new faith—is in Circumstance as *not* making impossible the individual's determination of his destiny." It is, we may say, Crane's vision of normality, a mind turned outward upon the world, away from its own crippling presentiments. The Easterner's epilogue, as it gestures inward towards an infinity of secret causes, is Crane's cry of resignation.

MARSTON LaFRANCE

"The Open Boat"

Crane students generally agree that "The Open Boat" (published June 1897) is "the crown of all his work," the one story which "would, even if he had written nothing else, have placed him where he now undoubtedly stands," an "impressionist masterpiece." Crane originally subtitled it a "tale intended to be after the fact," and Ralph D. Paine claimed that soon after the sinking of the *Commodore* he heard Crane read parts of the first draft to Captain Ed Murphy in Jacksonville "to get it right." The important parts of the story are indeed after the fact, not the fact itself, which Crane immediately dashed off for the newspapers in prose "as lifeless as the copy of a police court reporter," and nothing more clearly illustrates the essential insignificance of external fact in a Crane story than a comparison of "The Open Boat" with his own news report of the disaster. Yet a sentence near the end of his report— "The history of life in an open boat for thirty hours would no doubt be instructive for the young, but none is to be told here and now" —indicates that Crane had already seized upon that part of his adventure which "suited the purposes of his art, for 'The Open Boat' begins precisely where the newspaper account ends. It is clear . . . that the writer made his selection almost immediately." The report conveys the literal truth of the fact; Crane's structure imposed upon the fact in the work of art conveys the moral truth of the human experience; and the moral truth, in this story, becomes his "most powerful statement of the 'Crane world' and thus the most effective presentation of the stoic humanist theme."

The four men riding the waves in their ten-foot dinghy are obviously

From *A Reading of Stephen Crane.* © 1971 by Oxford University Press. Clarendon, 1971.

worried about capsizing and drowning at any moment because "each froth-top was a problem in small-boat navigation;" and, as several readers have noted, Crane exploits this constant threat by alternating, for purposes of contrast, the point of view from within the boat with that of a detached—and unthreatened—observer: "Viewed from a balcony, the whole thing would doubtless have been weirdly picturesque. But the men in the boat had no time to see it, and even if they had had leisure, there were other things to occupy their minds." Even a careless reading will reveal that, beginning with the ninth brief paragraph of the second section, one of the principal thoughts occupying their minds centres on an unknown experience (unknown at least to the correspondent through whose mind the story is transmitted) which they all realize will soon have to be undergone: the extremely dangerous business of passing through the surf to reach land. Crane leaves no doubt that this coming experience is a main concern: the surf and its hazards are mentioned at least fifteen times before the boat swamps and the men enter into their unavoidable action. Given this focus for the thoughts of the men, the story acquires a strong sense of movement and progression even at the surface level of physical action: the men relax when they first near the shore, and they even light cigars in expectation of being rescued soon, but when no boat comes, their sense of security changes to renewed fear of the impossible surf, and they return to sea to spend a dismal night in comparative safety; then, in the morning, when they finally resolve to attempt the surf unaided, the tension mounts steadily—for the reader but not, as will be seen, for the men themselves—as they wait for their boat to sink beneath them. Earlier, however, they fear this coming experience, and they formulate certain thoughts which reassure them and thus brace them to undergo it. To emphasize both the thoughts themselves and their psychological function, Crane presents them in the form of an incantation:

> If I am going to be drowned—if I am going to be drowned—if I am going to be drowned, why, in the name of the seven mad gods who rule the sea, was I allowed to come thus far and contemplate sand and trees? [This much of the incantation is given three times.] Was I brought here merely to have my nose dragged away as I was about to nibble the sacred cheese of life? It is preposterous. If this old ninny-woman, Fate, cannot do better than this, she should be deprived of the management of men's fortunes. . . . But no; she cannot mean to drown me. She dare not drown me. She cannot drown me. Not after all this work.
>
> (*Work,* 12, 41)

Then Crane immediately underscores the illusory nature of these thoughts by ending the paragraph with cutting irony: "Afterward the man might have had an impulse to shake his fist at the clouds. 'Just you drown me, now, and then hear what I call you!' " Nevertheless, the incantation recurs to the men as they await the inevitable, and the same illusion is stated in another fashion: "It was certainly an abominable injustice to drown a man who had worked so hard, so hard. The man felt it would be a crime most unnatural." Normally such notions are pierced and deflated by the climactic experience of the unknown.

In this story, however, Crane varies his pattern by making it set forth gradually the moral truth he wishes to communicate. The terrible night spent in the open boat prolongs their ordeal so long that awareness comes to the men *before* their encounter with the surf; this is the only Crane story in which both the protagonist's fears and illusions are dissipated, in which he attains the full awareness typical of the intelligent man after the fact of experience, before the feared unknown is undergone. The illusory notions cease about one-third of the way through section six when the protagonist "knows the pathos of his situation," and he immediately recalls the soldier of the Legion dying in Algiers. He is fully aware of nature's indifference before the boat swamps, knows that his extremity is at "the grave-edge," and "it merely occurred to him that if he should drown it would be a shame." When he is trapped in the current he thinks only "I am going to drown? Can it be possible? Can it be possible?" And before the boat swamps, Crane explicitly states that the men have conquered their fear: "The correspondent, observing the others, knew that they were not afraid. . . . There were no hurried words, no pallor, no plain agitation"; and the correspondent himself is so weary that he "did not care." When the men are finally dumped into the surf the injured captain clings to the overturned dinghy and is swept in to shore; the cook in his life preserver paddles himself in with one of the oars; the correspondent, also with part of a life preserver, has a comparatively easy task of swimming to shore after being trapped temporarily in a particular current; but the oiler, physically the best man of them all, is drowned at the last moment. The only response his death evokes in the others is implicitly a mature, calm acceptance: there are no "shrill, seething sentences," no bursts of "tupenny fury" at fate or external nature, nothing but the quiet acknowledgment that for the body of the oiler the land's welcome can only be the grave. Their comrade's death brings no great revelation to the others because they have already come to an awareness, before abandoning the boat, that a man can drown a few feet off shore as readily as any number of miles out at sea, that both his comparative fitness to survive and the amount of work he has done are irrelevant to this simple truth, and that man's moral realities of justice or injustice have no application whatsoever to external nature. The story ends with the famous line, "they felt that they could then [i.e., after undergoing their whole experience, including their brother's death] be interpreters." However, because the subject of their interpretation is "the great sea's voice" which the little shell tried to interpret to the pines, because they can now interpret to man his real role in the midst of amoral nature, Crane's variation of his psychological pattern causes this story to open outwards, as it were, to set forth the moral norm implied by the poems. Crane's world view and the stoic humanism it demands of man gradually emerge as the protagonist's fear and illusion give way to his deepening awareness of reality. And this protagonist is no untried youth to begin with. "He is represented as an experienced, cynical, somewhat dogmatic individual. His initiation is not into manhood, as is Fleming's, but into a new attitude towards nature and his fellow-men."

Scholars disagree over the role of nature: Greenfield claims that nature "is *the* antagonist" in this story; Mrs. Lang (by way of Emerson) and R. P. Adams (by way of Whitman) argue that man's unity with nature is the lesson learned by the interpreters; and, of course, others offer the naturalistic doctrine that nature as an overwhelming, mechanical, and indifferent force "raises a question, not only about the ultimate value of heroic behavior, but even about the possibility of its existence." Yet Crane at least tries to be precise in his statement. External nature in "The Open Boat," as in all Crane's work, is neither cruel, "nor beneficent, nor treacherous, nor wise. But she was indifferent, flatly indifferent." Hence, if chance or human error brings a man into so precarious a situation that he desires "to confront a personification and indulge in pleas, bowed to one knee, and with hands supplicant, saying 'Yes, but I love myself' " his answer will not be reassuring: "A high cold star on a winter's night is the word he feels that she says to him. Thereafter he knows the pathos of his situation." Logically, the last depth of this pathos—man's utter moral loneliness in the universe—is probably his realization that nature's absolute indifference precludes even antagonism. Although man's weak mental machinery may perceive external nature differently under different circumstances . . . —as indeed Crane's manipulation of point of view in this very story illustrates—this externality is inevitably a moral blank, a fixed condition of being. And in Crane's world any transcendental unity achieved by moral man with amoral nature is the illusion of an innocent:

> The belief that the individual can reach at least a partial understanding of the human condition in relation to external nature—that he can "interpret" nature—is not necessarily a romantic notion;

it is eminently classical. The romantic "solution" to the problem is a mystical union with . . . natural forces, so that the questions are not answered; they merely dissolve in intuitive understanding . . . The classical view is that nature is truly "external," at least to those attributes which differentiate man as man; knowledge, and a conscious choice of action based upon that knowledge, is man's only guide through the labyrinth of nature, even though the knowledge is always partial. Whatever unity exists is predicated upon the common humanity which the individual shares with humankind.

The fact that man's moral identification with his fellow man is independent of external nature has to mean that externality, no matter how unsuitable to human life it may occasionally become, raises no questions about either the possibility of heroic behaviour or its ultimate value in the moral world of man: "The belief that courage is a reality is not proved when a wave rescues the correspondent or disproved when another wave drowns the oiler. Man's values are defined *in* actuality, but they are not defined *by* actuality." Hence, one of the best readings that this story has received claims "a slowly changing three-fold view of nature which is revealed in the characters' thoughts: they see nature first as malevolently hostile, then as thoughtlessly hostile, and finally as wholly indifferent. This progress of ideas also accompanies the men's deepening concept of brotherhood." Because the protagonist of Crane's pattern always works his way to awareness of a reality that was available to him before his psychological journey began, and because Crane altered his pattern in "The Open Boat" to bring this awareness to his protagonist gradually, the *moral* reality of brotherhood in this story emerges roughly in three stages to correspond with the gradual disintegration of the protagonist's illusions as he becomes increasingly aware of the *physical* reality of indifferent nature.

The first commitment is made by each to the others within the boat; and the story implies that this sense of brotherhood arose almost immediately because, by the time it is mentioned (at the beginning of the third section), the correspondent's awareness of it is well after the fact. When a man suddenly finds himself adrift in an open boat his first impression of the surrounding sea will emphasize the danger which confronts him. The mutual commitment within the group, like the brotherhood of the Regulars, is each man's moral answer of selfless cooperation in the boat to counteract the threatening physical forces outside it as effectively as possible with their united effort. Thus, most of the attributes of this particular commitment—the awareness of danger as its immediate cause, its expression only in action, its lack of explicit acknowledgment, its respect for authoritative command, its significance beyond the demands of mere duty—were soon to reappear in Crane's analysis of the Regulars' code:

> It would be difficult to describe the subtle brotherhood of men that was here established on the seas. No one said that it was so. No one mentioned it. But it dwelt in the boat, and each man felt it warm him . . . and they were friends—friends in a more curiously iron-bound degree than may be common. The hurt captain . . . could never command a more ready and swiftly obedient crew. . . . It was more than a mere recognition of what was best for the common safety. There was surely in it a quality that was personal and heart-felt. And after this devotion to the commander of the boat, there was this comradeship, that the correspondent, for instance, who had been taught to be cynical of men, knew even at the time was the best experience of his life. But no one said that it was so. No one mentioned it.

This group feeling within the boat is emphasized by the appearance of the shark when the correspondent believes himself to be the only man awake. Although companionship will not preserve a man from a shark, "he did not wish to be alone with the thing. He wished one of his companions to awake by chance and keep him company with it."

After the men have been so long in the same danger that the threat has lost its edge for them—after "their backbones had become thoroughly used to balancing in the boat" —they begin to think beyond their immediate predicament: the oiler observes that "None of those other boats could have got ashore to give word of the wreck." When night comes, the symbolic universality of their situation is forcefully presented by the image of enveloping darkness in which two lights, the creations of man, "were the furniture of the world." Shortly afterwards, the thoughts which herald the collapse of the men's illusions are presented: "When it occurs to a man that nature does not regard him as important, and that she feels she would not maim the universe by disposing of him, he at first wishes to throw bricks at the temple, and he hates deeply the fact that there are no bricks and no temples." Such a passage marks a transitional state: such verbs as "regard," "feels," and "dispose," like the personal pronoun, imply the personification of the old ninny-woman; but the recognition that there are neither bricks nor temples leads straight to the depersonalized, remote indifference of the "high cold star on a winter's night." And with this image comes awareness of the pathos of the human situation. As implied by the poems, once a good man becomes aware of the universal human condition he will also perceive the moral demands his situation implicitly makes of him. Hence, as if "to chime the notes of his emotion," the correspondent identifies himself with, and feels compassion for, the dying soldier of the Legion toward whom previously he had been "perfectly *indifferent*" (italics mine). This earlier indifference resulted from the correspondent's innocence. His new sense of universal brotherhood derives from his "profound and perfectly impersonal comprehension" of man's plight. Thus, his former innocence and indifference should not only recall the people on the shore who saw the boat and did nothing, but also imply the crying need for aware interpreters of the great sea's voice.

This need is emphasized with the final stage of awareness which comes when the wind-tower, "a giant, standing with its back to the plight of the ants," represents, "to the correspondent, the serenity of nature amid the struggles of the individual—nature in the wind, and nature in the vision of men." The unalterable indifference of moral man; and the correspondent then realizes "the innumerable flaws of his life" and vows that, given another chance, he will "mend his conduct and his words, and be better and brighter during an introduction or at a tea." He vows that he will no longer be indifferent toward his fellow man even in the most banal situations, that he will wholeheartedly affirm even the social clichés by means of which human brotherhood can be expressed. The vast difference between the natural world and the moral world of man, implied through the image of the wind-tower, is stressed in the final scenes of the story. When the men approach the land with its cottages there is not a sign of life—not even a dog—to be seen; hence, they "contemplate the lonely and indifferent shore" which, without man, is as indifferent as the sea. This amorality is shattered when a man comes running down the beach flinging off his clothes to plunge into the sea "naked as a tree in winter" and help the men. To the correspondent "a halo was about his head, and he shone like a saint," but no Christian reference is implied by the context: this naked man is the first person to act towards the castaways as an aware moral being should, and his sainthood is earned in terms of his enthusiastic practice of simple humanity towards a suffering brother, specifically by "a strong pull, and a long drag, and a bully heave at the correspondent's hand." Then the indifferent shore is transformed: "instantly the beach was populated with men with blankets, clothes, and flasks, and women with coffee-pots and all the remedies sacred to their minds. The welcome of the land to the men from the sea [i.e., of aware humankind to the living men from the sea] was warm and generous." But the oiler is dead, and his death poignantly underlines the distinction: what remains—as in the final stanza of "A man adrift on a slim spar"—is no longer a part of the moral world of living man; thus, the land's welcome to the "still and dripping shape" can "only be" a lonely and indifferent grave. The human commitment to brotherhood in this story enlarges from the immediate group to universal mankind to the social forms man has created for communicating his humanity to other living men; and the whole progression, as in the poems, is offered as the logical corollary of man's alien position in an indifferent universe.

Three apparent misreadings deserve brief comment. The progress of the men in the boat is no romantic death and rebirth; they progressively acquire awareness—in the classic sense of gradual accomplishment through painful effort—of an already existing reality which is both physical (the indifference of nature) and moral (the necessary brotherhood of man). Similarly, nothing in the story suggests that the oiler is a Christ figure, or that his death is in any way sacrificial. The oiler does no more than the others to get the boat ashore: each man does his best, and if Billie is more capable than the others this mere physical distinction has to be ascribed to the chance grouping of these four men in the boat, not to his moral credit. Moreover, he has his full reward and enjoys it while still living, his active participation in the brotherhood, which is the best experience of life. When his death occurs the time of the common struggle of each for the good of all within the boat has passed, and each man in the surf has to fend for himself. The oiler is killed by mere chance, a death which could have come to any of the others with exactly the same significance in context. This death signifies the immense value of brotherhood among living men because, while contingency remains in externals, as Jumper puts it, the moral realities which make human life meaningful to the living are not in themselves contingent upon external effect:

> blind chance is of the essence of the material world. Only in the world of humanity is there the possibility of purposeful action. The sole remnant of theology that survives in Crane's world is the stoic human will. . . .A world view which cannot take such a contingency into account will ill prepare its holder for the realities of life.

Billie's death, in short, suggests that Crane's humanism is realistic, neither romantic nor sentimental. Finally, Crane's protagonist, the correspondent, is also his spokesman in this story. The correspondent's consciousness is the vehicle which transmits the story to the reader, his mental machinery copes with the external reality and develops the philosophical conclusions which derive from his chastening experience. There is no irony aimed at his position to undermine his authority for the reader—the rescuer dashing down the sand should legitimately appear "like a saint" to the exhausted correspondent—and Crane himself, in several stories and poems, obviously affirms both the view of external nature and the moral commitment that his spokesman here brings to the reader.

To be an "interpreter" of the great sea's voice to man is to "teach," with the "gold of patience," the "gospel of gentle hands." Crane's tale after the fact documents the human position in an unfeeling universe where man's presence is an accident; and thus it "cries a brotherhood of hearts" as a necessity for man's very existence in this eternally open boat.

ALAN TRACHTENBERG

Experiments in Another Country: Stephen Crane's City Sketches

In 1894 Crane published a number of city stories and sketches in the daily press in New York. He thought well enough of these experimental pieces to consider collecting them as "Midnight Sketches." Considering their origins as newspaper sketches, these mainly short, deft impressions of New York street life seem more like apprentice work than finished inventions. One of the reasons for their interest is, however, exactly the fact of their having been produced for the press as newspaper performances. If the stories show the young writer, still in his early twenties, experimenting with language to develop an appropriate style, the newspaper itself must be taken into account as a given of the experimental situation. Crane derived the form itself, the "sketch," from the newspaper, and at a deeper level the form provided a challenge, a barrier to be overcome.

The big city daily, especially as it developed in the 1890s, has its *raison d'être* chiefly in the mystification of urban space, a mystification it claims to dispel as "news" yet simultaneously abets as "sensationalism." The newspaper addresses itself abstractly to a "public" which is the collective identity each isolated urban consciousness is invited to join, a neutral space held in common as the negation of hidden private space. The motive of the metropolitan press, Robert Park writes, is "to reproduce as far as possible, in the city, the conditions of life in the village." In villages "everyone knew everyone else, everyone called everyone by his first name." The tactic of searching out "human interest," of making the commonplace seem picturesque or dramatic, is an attempt to fill the distances inherent in mystified space with formulaic emotion fostering the illusion of distance transcended. In their daily recurrence newspapers express concretely the estrangement of an urban consciousness

From *The Southern Review* 10, no. 2 (April 1974). © 1974 by Alan Trachtenberg.

no longer capable of free intimacy with its own material life. In their form
the wish for the commonplace or the demystification of social distance coex-
ists with the wish not to dispel mystery, to retain as surrogate experience the
aura of awe, allurement, fear which surrounds street experience.

Crane was not an ordinary reporter on assignment; he wrote as a "literary"
observer, a personal reporter of city scenes. His sketches were not "news";
nor were they entirely fiction, though he was capable of "making up" an account of a fire which never occurred and placing it in the New York *Press*
as a signed report. The sketches present themselves as personal reports from
and on *experience,* frankly colored by a personal style. The convention of
such stylized reporting already existed in New York journalism as an expression of the newspapers' need to transform random street experience into *someone's* experience. The convention provided Crane with an opportunity to
cultivate an authentic style as a vehicle of personal vision. The danger was
that pressure to distinguish his vision, to make his signature recognizable,
would lead to stylization.

Choosing themes familiar to newspaper, magazine, and novel readers,
Crane developed a distinctive manner, a kind of notation which rendered
physical scenes in highlighted color and sound. "When Everyone Is Panic-
stricken," his fire report hoax, opens:

> We were walking on one of the shadowy side streets west of Sixth
> Avenue. The midnight silence and darkness was upon it save where
> at the point of intersection with the great avenue there was a broad
> span of yellow light. From there came the steady monotonous jingle
> of streetcar bells and the weary clatter of hooves on the cobbles.
> While the houses in this street turned black and mystically silent
> with the night the avenue continued its eternal movement and life,
> a great vein that never slept nor paused. The gorgeous orange-
> hued lamps of the saloon flared plainly and the figures of some
> loungers could be seen as they stood on the corner. Passing to and
> fro the tiny black figures of people made an ornamental border
> on this fabric of yellow light.

The effect is painterly, precise, impressionistic. Crane's eye for detail, his ability
to take in a scene and convey its sense, its contours, in a few telling strokes,
suggest important correspondence between his visual intentions and that of
impressionist painters and photographers. The notation here, and typically
in the city sketches, seizes a passing moment and formalizes it as a picture
drawn from a precise physical perspective—from the shadowy side street
toward the great avenue and its gorgeous yellow light. Within the formalization

the scene contains motion, the potential for change, for the appearance of the sudden and the unexpected. The potency is held in the carefully constructed spatial relation between the black, silent houses in "this street" and the unsleeping, flaring life of the avenue. The relation has, moreover, the potential of an ironic contrast, one which does in fact emerge as the "grim midnight reflection upon existence" of the narrator and his companion (identified only as "the stranger"), "in the heavy shadows and in the great stillness" of the street, are disputed by a sudden "muffled cry of a woman" from one of the "dark impassive houses" and the "sound of the splinter and crash of broken glass, falling to the pavement." The pictorial patterns of the opening paragraph give way to the frenzy and excitement of a midnight fire. Like the shadowy street itself the stranger suddenly flares into life, clutches the narrator's arm, drags him to the blazing house, himself a mirror of its vehemence. Through his responses Crane registers the effective transformation of the scene from shadow to blaze, from grimness to frenzy: "The stranger's hand tightened convulsively on my arm, his enthusiasm was like the ardor of one who looks upon the pageantry of battles. 'Ah, look at 'em! look at 'em! ain't that great?' " The spatial relations and contrasts of the opening picture contain, in short, visual elements corresponding to the little drama which this fake news story performs.

A similar dramatization of visual detail and spatial relations to deepen and complicate conventional newspaper action appears in many of the sketches. Their interest lies in the fact that Crane used the occasion—the "personal" or "feature" reporter in search of copy—to develop techniques for rendering events on city streets as unique and complex experiences. Defining his literary problem from within such conventions posed certain difficulties; literalism, sensationalism, sentimentality were the ogres of the newspaper story Crane had to slay in his own work. From within the conventions Crane was able to discover a ground for genuine creation. That ground lay chiefly within the spatial structure of the common city story. Crane grasped the element of *mystery* within that structure and made it the basis of his point of view.

The most prominent and sensational of the spatial images in this period was that of the "other half," represented by the maze of streets and alleys and courtyards in lower Manhattan. In his famous exposures of living conditions in the slums, Jacob Riis, reporter for the New York *Sun,* excavated place names like Mulberry Bend, Bottle Alley, and Bandit's Roost. These names joined the "Bowery" as signals of forbidding and exotic territory. Illustrating his stories and books with photographs that explored to the "darkest corner," Riis established a pattern of spatial penetration which provided his readers with various expeditions into mysterious quarters. His technique was that of a guided tour; his aim, to convert the reader from passive ignorance to active awareness and caring. In the sensations of his disclosures lurks some residue of the city *mystery.*

> Leaving the Elevated Railroad where it dives under the Brooklyn Bridge at Franklin Square, scarce a dozen steps will take you where we wish to go . . . with its rush and roar echoing yet in our ears we have turned the corner from prosperity to poverty. We stand upon the domain of the tenement. . . . enough of them everywhere. Suppose we look into one? No. — Cherry Street. Be a little careful, please! the hall is dark and you might stumble over the children pitching pennies there. Not that it would hurt them; kicks and cuffs are their daily diet. They have little else. Here where the hall turns and dives into utter darkness is a step and another, another, a flight of stairs. You can feel your way, if you cannot see it. Close? Yes! What would you have? All the fresh air that ever enters these stairs comes from the hall door that is forever slamming and from the windows of dark bedrooms that in turn we see from the stairs the sole supply of the elements God meant to be free, but that man deals out with such niggardly hand.

And so on. The strategy is to place the reader in a moral relation of outrage, indignation, or pity. But it remains a touristic device; the reader is not permitted to cross into the inner world of the slums—into its own point of view— and see the outer world from that perspective. The moral stance which defines the "other half" as "problem" assures distance.

The portrayal of "low life" in much of the popular writing of the period employed analogous devices to preserve distance—devices of picturesque perspective or sentimental plot which protected the reader from the danger of a true exchange of point of view with the "other half." The danger appears as such in an interesting passage in an essay on "New York Streets" by William Dean Howells. In his walks through the "wretched quarters," he writes, he permits himself to become "hardened, for the moment, to the deeply underlying fact of human discomfort" by indulging himself in the "picturesqueness" of the scene: "The sidewalks swarm with children and the air rings with clamor as they fly back and forth at play; on the thresholds the mothers sit nursing their babes and the old women gossip together," etc. He remarks then, shrewdly, that "in a picture it would be most pleasingly effective, for then you could be in it and yet have the distance on it which it needs." To be *in it,* however, is "to inhale the stenches of the neglected street and to catch that yet fouler and dreadfuler poverty-smell which breed from the open doorways. It is to see the children quarreling in their games and beating each other in the face and rolling each other in the gutter like the little savage outlaws they are." This reality, if you are a walker in the city, "makes you hasten your pace down to the river" and escape. The passage confesses at once to the denials of the picturesque view and the offensiveness of an unmediated view.

How then was "low life" to be viewed? For Howells, Riis, and for many concerned writers, a moral posture supplied the necessary screen of protection from an exchange of subjectivities. But the possibility of such an exchange—indeed its necessity if the logic of the convention were to complete itself—is implicit in the spatial pattern. It is precisely this possibility that Crane recognized in his city sketches—a possibility which provides the formal structure of two of the most ambitious of the city stories, the companion pieces "Experiment in Misery" and "Experiment in Luxury," and which illuminate his stylistic intentions throughout the sketches. Already in *Maggie: A Girl of the Streets* (1893) and *George's Mother* (presumably composed in 1894, in the same period of the city sketches), Crane had discarded the moral posture of the tourist and had tried to convey physical landscapes equivalent to his perception of the subjective lives of his characters. His materials for *Maggie* seem to have been derived almost entirely from written accounts of the lives of slum people by investigators like Riis and the evangelist T. Dewitt Talmage. The story is, in effect, a retelling of a familiar plot: Maggie (the name itself was virtually generic), pure blossom of the slums, driven by indifference, selfishness, sexual exploitation, first to streetwalking then to suicide in the East River. For Crane the plot was an occasion for him to tell a familiar tale with vividness, with exactness of observation, and most of all, with sufficient irony to make it apparent that the characters themselves viewed their world melodramatically, through lenses blurred with the same false emotions they inspired—as "low life" —in the many popular tellers of their tale. Crane aims at accuracy, not compassion. The story is a complicated piece of parody written with a serious regard for the task of rendering a false tale truly. Crane's version of "low life," in *George's Mother* as well as *Maggie,* aims to represent the subjectivities of his characters. Each of the characters in these two novellas lives inwardly in a withdrawn psychic space, possessed by the shadowy feelings and escapist yearnings of the city's popular culture. Each is self-deceived, estranged from all others, occupying an imaginative world of his own.

Crane's recognition of the "mosaic of little worlds" and its demands upon representation is manifest in one of the best-known of the street sketches, "The Men in the Storm." The sketch is of a crowd of homeless men observed on the street during a blizzard as they wait with growing impatience and dangerous discontent for the "doors of charity" to open. Images of the homeless and jobless waiting for charity on the street were common in the writing and graphics of the period. Crane's piece differs from the standard treatment in several crucial ways. It is not a social study; it neither excites compassion for the men nor induces social guilt in the reader for their plight. It is a rendering of a scene, a depiction of a space, as objective as Alfred Stieglitz's street photographs with a hand-held camera in the same year. Crane's concern is with the phenomenon before him and his writing is almost surgical in its sureness of stroke. He writes to achieve an accurate statement of the feeling of the scene and his details are physical correlatives of the men's feelings of pitiless cold, biting wind, and snow that "cut like knives and needles." The men are driven by the storm "like sheep in a winter's gale." Viewed from without, they are also seen as possessing a collective subjectivity. For example, in their fierce condition they still can swear "not like dark assassins, but in a sort of American fashion grimly and desperately it is true but yet with a wondrous undereffect definable and mystic as if there were some kind of humor in this catastrophe, in this situation in a night of snow-laden winds."

A picture of a desperate scene—of men subjected to cold wind, snow, and hunger, alternately clinging to each other for warmth and fighting with each other for shelter—the sketch is also a highly pointed study in the problematics of point of view. Drawn from a detached floating perspective, the sketch contains several limited points of view, each located spatially and each characterized by a feeling linked to its space. The opening paragraphs present a picture of late afternoon busy streets as the blizzard begins to swirl upon pedestrians and drivers of vehicles and horses. The mood is grim at first: people are huddled, drivers are furious, horses slip and strain; "overhead the trains rumbled and roared and the dark structure of the elevated railroad stretching over the avenue dripped little streams and drops of water upon the mud and snow beneath it." But the next paragraph introduces a more hopeful note. The perspective shifts momentarily to an interior, "to one who looked from a window"; the clatter of the streets, softened by snow, "becomes important music, a melody of life made necessary to the ear by the dreariness of the pitiless beat and sweep of the storm." The warmth of the interior in which such musings are likely pervades the paragraph; the shop windows, "aglow with light," are "infinitely cheerful," and now "the pace of the people and the vehicles" has a "meaning": "Scores of pedestrians and drivers wretched with cold faces, necks and feet, speeding for scores of unknown doors and entrances, scattering to an infinite variety of shelters, to places which the imagination made warm with the colors of home." The objective scene has been constructed to reveal a subjective mood—the storm is pitiless but the imagination warms itself with images of doors, entrances, home: "There was an absolute expression of hot dinners in the pace of the people." Crane then introduces a conjectural point of view inspired by the scene: "If one dared to speculate upon the destination of those who came trooping, he lost himself in a maze of social calculations. He might fling a handful of sand and attempt to follow the flight of each particular grain." But the entire troop has in common the thought of hot dinners: "It is a matter of tradition; it is from the tales of childhood. It comes forth with every storm." Social calculation might be pleasant, diversionary, but trivial. All classes are reduced to those who speed home in the blizzard warmed with the thoughts of food, and those who do not. At this point Crane performs the sketch's most decisive modulation of perspective: "However, in a certain part of the dark West side street, there was a collection of men to whom these things were as if they were not." The stark negative halts all calculation.

The narrator has subtly worked upon the reader's point of view, freeing it from the hold of customary feeling so that it might receive freely a newly discovered "moral region," the territory of "half darkness" in which occurs another kind of existence. In the description which follows Crane twice again introduces a shift in perspective in order to confirm better the spatial independence of his own. At one point, across the street from the huddled men, the figure of a stout, well-dressed man appears "in the brilliantly lighted space" of the shop window. He observes the crowd, stroking his whiskers: "It seemed that the sight operated inversely, and enabled him to more clearly regard his own environment, delightful relatively." The man's complacency is echoed at the end of the sketch as the narrator notes a change in expression in the features of the men as they near the receiving door of charity: "As they thus stood upon the threshold of their hopes they looked suddenly content and complacent, the fire had passed from their eyes and the snarl had vanished from their lips. The very force of the crowd in the rear which had previously vexed them was regarded from another point of view, for it now made it inevitable that they should go through the little doors into the place that was cheery and warm with light."

By projecting in the contrasted points of view a dialectic of felt values, Crane forces the reader to free his own point of view from any limiting perspective. Crane thus transforms the conventional event of turning corners and crossing thresholds into a demanding event: a change of perspective which as its prerequisite recapitulates a number of limited perspectives. Crane's "Men in the Storm" differs, for example, from a characteristic "literary" treatment of the same theme such as Howells's "The Midnight Platoon" by its achievement of a point of view superior to, yet won through a negation of, perspectives limited by social, moral, or aesthetic standards. Howells's piece concerns a breadline as it is perceived from a carriage by a man who comes to recognize himself as comfortable and privileged. The figure in the story approaches the scene as a "connoisseur of such matters," enjoying the anticipation of "the pleasure of seeing"; he wants to "glut his sensibility in a leisurely study of the scene." The breadline is to him "this representative thing" and he perceives in the crowd of hungry men "a fantastic association of their double files and those of the galley-slaves whom Don Quixote released." His mind wanders in conjecture:

> How early did these files begin to form themselves for the mid-night dole of bread? As early as ten, as nine o'clock? If so, did the fact argue habitual destitution, or merely habitual leisure? Did the slaves in the coffle make acquaintance, or remain strangers to one another, though they were closely neighbored night after night by their misery? Perhaps they joked away the weary hours of waiting; they must have their jokes. Which of them were old-comers, and which novices? Did they ever quarrel over questions of precedence? Had they some comity, some etiquette, which a man forced to leave his place could appeal to, and so get it back? Could one say to his next-hand man, "Will you please keep my place?" and would this man say to an interloper, "Excuse me, this place is engaged"? How was it with them, when the coffle worked slowly or swiftly past the door where the bread and coffee were given out, and word passed to the rear that the supply was ex-hausted? This must sometimes happen, and what did they do then?

Aware that the men look back at him with equal curiosity, he suddenly recognizes his own "representativity." To them, he realizes, he stands for Society, the Better Classes, and the literary picturesque notions dissolve as he feels himself face to face with the social issue. Howells here confronts the social distance, portrays it as filled with middle-class rationalization, and ends with a "problem": what are "we" to do about these men and their suffering?

For Crane, the question is as if it were not. He writes from a curiously asocial perspective—or, at least, a perspective disengaged from that of the typical middle-class viewer; he approximates (though he does not yet achieve) the perspective of the men. That is, what Howells sees as a thoroughly social matter of how the classes view each other, Crane sees as a technical problem: how to represent the scene before him. He is not concerned with converting the reader to social sympathy (perhaps distrustful or weary of the conde-scension of such a stance), but with converting the sheer data into *experience*.

He writes as a phenomenologist of the scene, intent on characterizing the consciousness of the place (which includes its separate points of view) by a rendering of felt detail. Each of Crane's images resonates with significance as a component of the episode's inner structure of feeling; the exactness of the correlation of detail to feeling leads, in fact, to the frequent mistake of describing Crane as a symbolist. His *realism,* however, in the phenomenological sense, points to the significance, indeed the radicalism, of these sketches. For Crane transforms a street scene, a passing sensation for which a cognitive mold is already prepared in his reader's eye, into a unique experience.

If, following Walter Benjamin, we require that works be "situated in the living social context," then the immediate context is that established by the author with his reader; it is in that relationship that the possibility of each becoming "real" and particular for the other exists. In this case, the relationship is mediated by the sketch's appearance in a newspaper, and at a deeper level, by its formal expression of the newspaper motive: a "human interest" observation on a street. But typically the newspaper does not permit its own formal qualities so intense and exact a realization. Newspapers respond, as I have pointed out, to the increasing mystification, the deepening estrangement of urban space from interpenetration, from exchange of subjectivities. But their response is to deepen the crisis while seeming to allay it. In their typographical form, their typical verbal usage, they serve, Benjamin writes, "to isolate what happens from the realm in which it could affect the experience of the reader." By isolating information from experience, moreover, they deaden the capacity of memory; the lack of connection among the data of the newspaper page reduces all items to the status of "today's events." The newspaper, Benjamin writes, "is the showplace of the unrestrained degradation of the word." In *War Is Kind* Crane wrote:

> A newspaper is a collection of half-injustices
> Which, bawled by boys from mile to mile,
> Spreads its curious opinion
> To a million merciful and sneering men,
> While families cuddle the joys of the fireside
> When spurred by tale of dire lone agony.
> A newspaper is a court
> Where every one is kindly and unfairly tried
> But a squalor of honest men.
> A newspaper is a market
> Where wisdom sells its freedom

And melons are crowned by the crowd.
A newspaper is a game
Where his error scores the player victory
While another's skill wins death.
A newspaper is a symbol;
It is fetless life's chronicle,
A collection of loud tales
Concentrating eternal stupidities
That in remote ages lived unhaltered,
Roaming through a fenceless world.

The poem expresses nicely Crane's recognition of the constricting function of the newspaper as a "market" in which are sold "loud tales" to a world that appears "fenced-in." He has no illusions about the newspaper and the degradation of literature it represents.

Yet, as Benjamin argues, within the logic of the newspaper lies a possible condition for the salvation of the word—in the new relationships it fosters between writer and world, between writer and reader. Crane accepted the condition of newspaper production and produced within it work which, with the complicity of his careful reader, converts the data of street life into memorable experience. He thus transvalues, or as Benjamin would put it, "alienates" the apparatus of production and forces his reader to become an accomplice, that is, to become himself an experimenter in mystified space. The best example among the sketches, an example which reveals Crane's motives almost diagrammatically, is the often misunderstood "Experiment in Misery." In this and in its companion piece, "Experiment in Luxury," published a week apart in the New York *Press*, Crane presents a figure, a "youth," who enters opposite social realms—in the first a seedy lodging house, in the second the mansion of a millionaire. The report in both cases is of the quality of life, of the awareness which inhabits each interior. The method in each "Experiment" is to convey the inner feeling by having the youth "try on" the way of life. The spaces are thus presumably demystified by the youth's assuming the point of view implicit in the physical structures and the actions of their interiors. For example, as he lounges with his rich friend, smoking pipes, the youth feels a sense of liberty unknown on the streets. "It was an amazing comfortable room. It expressed to the visitor that he could do supremely as he chose, for it said plainly that in it the author did supremely as he chose." Before long "he began to feel that he was a better man than many—entitled to a great pride." In each case the narrative point of view projects the youth's consciousness; he is made into a register of the world-as-it-is-felt of the particular setting. In this way Crane transmutes social fact into felt experience.

The stories are not identical in their strategies, however. Both begin with a frame in which the youth is encouraged by an older friend, in a conversation on a street, to undertake the experiment. As companion pieces they together confront the great division which was the popular mode through which "society" was perceived in the culture of the period: luxury and misery, rich and poor, high and low, privileged and underprivileged. Intentionally then, they comprise a social statement. In the "luxury" piece, unlike the other, Crane consciously works from a social proposition: his "experiment" is an attempt to discover if indeed the inner life of the very rich justifies the "epigram" "stuffed . . . down the throat" of the complaining poor by "theologians" that "riches did not bring happiness." The motive of the "misery" story is less overtly ideological: it is to learn of the "tramp" "how he feels." The narrative technique of the "luxury" story differs from the other in that the youth carries on his "experiment" along with a simultaneous inner dialogue based on observation and self-reflection. He learns that the rich do, after all, live pretty well, if insipidly. He could "not see that they had great license to be pale and haggard." The story assumes a point of view in order to shatter a social myth. Being rich makes a difference.

Discursive self-reflection plays no role in the companion sketch. In fact, to intensify attention on the experience itself, and to indicate that the social drama of displacing one's normal perspective already is internalized in the action, Crane discarded the opening and closing frames when he republished the story in a collection of 1898. In his revision he also added to the opening paragraphs a number of physical details which reinforce and particularize the sense of misery. Streetcars, which in the first version "rumbled softly, as if going on carpet stretched in the aisle made by the pillars of the elevated road," become a "silent procession . . . moving with formidable power, calm and irresistible, dangerous and gloomy, breaking silence only by the loud fierce cry of the gong." The elevated train station, now supported by "leg-like pillars," resembles "some monstrous kind of a crab squatting over the street." These revisions and others suggest an intention more fully realized: the creation of physical equivalents to the inner experience of a "moral region" of misery.

The first version makes clear that the youth's "experiment" is a conscious disguise in order to search out "experience." "Two men stood regarding a tramp," it opens; the youth "wonders" how he "feels" and is advised by his older friend that such speculations are "idle" (a finely ironic word, as is "regarding") unless he is "in" the tramp's condition. The youth agrees to "try" it: "Perhaps I could discover his point of view or something near it." The frame opens with an awareness, then, of what the older man calls "distance," and establishes "experiment" as a method of overcoming it. So far the situation recalls the wish of Howells's witness of the breadline to penetrate distance, as it does the situation in many similar down-and-out pieces in the period. For example, in *Moody's Lodging House and Other Tenement Sketches* (1895), also a collection of newspaper sketches, Alvan Francis Sanborn writes: "the best way to get at the cheap lodging-house life is to live it,—to get inside the lodging house and stay inside. For this, unless one possesses a mien extraordinarily eloquent of roguery or misery, or both, a disguise is helpful." Crane's youth borrows a disguise from the "studio of an artist friend" (this suggestive detail is dropped in the revised version), and begins his experiment: as Crane puts it with a note of irony, the youth "went forth." The irony is directed at the hint of naive chivalric adventuresomeness in the youth and prepares for the authentic conversion of his subjective life to follow.

In what follows the youth proceeds downtown in the rain; he is "plastered with yells of 'bum' and 'hobo' " by small boys, he is wet and cold, and "he felt that there no longer could be pleasure in life." In City Hall Park he feels the contrast between himself and the homeward bound "well-dressed Brooklyn people" and he proceeds further "down Park Row" where "in the sudden descent in the style of the dress of the crowd he felt relief, and as if he were at last in his own country" (this last significant detail was added in the revision). The youth begins to inhabit this other country, first by occupying himself with "the pageantry of the street," then "caught by the delectable sign," allowing himself to be "swallowed" by a "voracious" looking saloon door advertising "free hot soup." His descent deepens. The next step is to find someone with "a knowledge of cheap lodging houses," and he finds his man in a seedy character "in strange garments" with a strange guilty look about his eyes, a look which earns him the youth's epithet of "assassin." The youth confesses himself also a "stranger" and follows the lead of his companion to a "joint" of "dark and secret places" from which assail him "strange and unspeakable odors." The interior is "black, opaque" and during the night the youth lies sleepless as the dormitory takes on the grim appearance of a fiendish morgue. Near him lies a man asleep with partly open eyes, his arm hanging over the cot, his fingers "full length upon the wet cement floor of the room." The spirit of the place seems contained in this image. "To the youth it seemed that he and the corpse-like being were exchanging a prolonged stare and that the other threatened with his eyes." The "strange effect of the graveyard" is broken suddenly by "long wails" that "dwindle to final melancholy moans" expressing "a red and grim tragedy of the unfathomable possibilities of the man's dreams." The youth feels now that he has penetrated to the deepest recesses of the tramp's condition.

But at this point Crane performs an important act of distancing the narrative from the point of view of the youth. Fulfilling the earlier hints of his naïveté, Crane now has the youth interpret the shrieks of the "vision pierced man" as "protest," as "an impersonal eloquence, with a strength not from him, giving voice to the wail of a whole section, a class, a people." An ideological romance settles in his mind, "weaving into the young man's brain and mingling with his views of these vast and sombre shadows," and he "lay carving biographies for these men from his meager experience." With morning and sunlight comes the "rout of the mystic shadows," however, and the youth sees that "daylight had made the room comparatively common-place and uninteresting." The men joke and banter as they dress, and some reveal in their nakedness that they were "men of brawn" until they put on their "ungainly garments." The normalization of feeling in this morning scene is crucial. When the youth reaches the street he "experienced no sudden relief from unholy atmospheres. He had forgotten all about them, and had been breathing naturally and with no sensation of discomfort or distress." The respiratory detail confirms the point; he is now indeed in his own country, where he might feel after breakfast that "B'Gawd, we've been livin' like kings." In the expansive moment his companion "brought forth long tales" about himself which reveal him as a confirmed hobo, always cadging and running from work. Together they make their way to City Hall Park, the youth now one of "two wanderers" who "sat down in a little circle of benches sanctified by traditions of their class." In the normalcy of his behavior he shows that his experience of misery, since the night before, has become less meager.

The story closes as the youth on the bench becomes aware of a new substance in his perceptions. Well-dressed people on the street give him "no gaze" and he feels "the infinite distance" from "all that he valued. Social position, comfort, the pleasures of living, were unconquerable kingdoms." His new world and theirs were separate countries. The separateness is discovered as a difference in perspective, in how the world is seen, felt, and accepted. Now, the tall buildings in the background of the park are "of pitiless hues and sternly high." They stand "to him" as emblems "of a nation forcing its regal head into the clouds, throwing no downward glances." "The roar of the city" is now "to him" a "confusion of strange tongues." Estrangement has become his own experience, no longer a "thought" about the original object of his perception, the tramp. The youth, and through him the reader, has attained an experimental point of view expressed in an act of the eyes in the concluding sentences: "He confessed himself an outcast, and his eyes from under the lowered rim of his hat began to glance guiltily, wearing the cirminal expression that comes with certain convictions." The conviction itself, of being excluded by the overarching buildings, accounts for the new perspective.

The two "experiments" conclude that the rich are banal but live well, and that the homeless poor are victims whose inner acquiescence is a form of cowardice. More important than such "meanings" are the strategies compressed in the word "experiment." In these strategies lie the specifically urban character of Crane's writings, a character which is his calculated invention out of the materials of the newspaper culture. Crane's "experiments" implicate Zola's but go beyond them. In the misery sketch "experiment" denotes the subject as well as the method; the sketch is "about" the youth's experiment, an anatomizing of the components of the naturalist's enterprise of investigating human life in its social habitat. But Crane is concerned with the investigator, with the exercise of the logic of investigation upon his subjectivity. The experiment transforms the youth, and it is through that transformatiom that the life of the city's strangers become manifest. The youth is transformed only provisionally, however; he is not converted, not reclassified as a tramp. His experiment is literally a trying-out, a donning of a costume in order to report on its fit and feel. In order to live provisionally as a stranger in another country he must have estranged himself even more deeply to begin with, that is, he must already have disengaged himself from all possible identities, from social identity as such. Crane recognized that the inner form of the newspaper culture was itself "experiment" and to fulfill its logic of disengagement was a prerequisite for recovering "experience" from the flux of the street. Crane's city sketches are "experimental" writing in the sense, finally, that they confront the transformation of literary relations (the writer's relation to his subject and to his reader) implicit in the big city's mystification of social and psychic space; they invent stylistic procedures for re-creating the word as experience.

Crane's direction was a descent to the street and to the constricted vision which lay there as broken images. Out of these he forged a unifying image of his own, a vision of a city peopled by nameless, desolate creatures, strangers to each other and to their own worlds. "The inhabitant of the great urban centers," writes Paul Valéry, "reverts to a state of savagery—that is, of isolation. The feeling of being dependent on others, which used to be kept alive by need, is gradually blunted in the smooth functioning of the social mechanism. Any improvement of this mechanism eliminates certain modes of behavior and emotions." Crane's vision is of a world already confirmed in its isolation, a world shocking in the absence of those "certain modes of behavior and emotion" which make subjective experience possible. The exchange of subjectivity performed by the youth rarely occurs among the characters of his city fiction; instead, violence always threatens as the promise of heightened sensation in defiance of the blunting mechanisms: a wail, a scream, a fire, a clutched arm. Crane's city people seem always ignitable, verging toward the discharge of feeling in riot. His own narrative point of view remains cool and aloof, however; his spatial penetrations end at the edge of sympathetic identification. Unlike Theodore Dreiser, he was little interested in character, little interested in exploring the versions of reality his style transcends. The expense of his expert technicianship was the larger novelistic vision Dreiser achieved. Dreiser also descended to the popular, to the banal, but the points of view of his characters were not provisional guises; he took them as self-sufficient acts of desire. Dreiser's city is a theme as well as a place: a magnet that attracts. Less than a place, Crane's city lies in the structured passages of his point of view; it is situated in his technique, in its processes of disengagement and recovery. His sketches are experiments in reading the "elsewhere" of the street.

JAMES   NAGEL

Stephen Crane
and the Narrative Methods
of Impressionism

In 1935, Ford Madox Ford, in looking back on the development of literary
Impressionism in fiction, wrote

> but it was perhaps [Stephen] Crane of all that school or gang—
> and not excepting Maupassant—who most observed that canon
> of Impressionism— "you must render: never report." You must
> never, that is to say, write: "He saw a man aim a gat at him": you
> must put it: "He saw a steel ring directed at him."

Ford's comment is a useful point of departure for exploring Crane's Impressionism and his handling of narration, for it implies a dramatic literature which
renders direct sensory experience without expository intrusion, without
authorial addition or correction. No intermediary intelligence asserts the existence of a gun in Ford's passage; the reader must interpret the sensory data
himself.

Indeed, narrative method is an especially important consideration for
writers within the Impressionistic mode, for their concern with vision, with
sensory experience, and with the apprehension of reality led to a new emphasis on the control of point of view. The fundamental method of Impressionism is the presentation of sensation so as to create the effect of immediate
sensory experience, a device which places the reader at the same epistemological position in the scene as the character involved. The qualifying
variable in this method is the determination of the human intelligence which
receives the sensations, a matter not operative in Impressionistic painting

From *Studies in the Novel* 10, no. 1 (Spring 1978). © 1978 by North Texas State
University.

and music because those forms proceed on the assumption that it is the artist or composer who does the perceiving. But fiction involves a formulating center of intelligence, a narrator who, in Impressionism, projects not what *he* perceives but what is apprehended and understood by one or more of the characters. The effect is a distancing from the author, a sensory objectivity which requires extraordinary skill in establishing verisimilitude.

Stephen Crane's success in rendering the effect of actual life was perhaps sufficiently established by the British reviewers of *The Red Badge of Courage,* who, assuming they were enjoying "slice of life" Realism, went on to assert that only someone who had personally experienced the events could have presented them so vividly. Sydney Brooks went so far as to say that if the novel "were altogether a work of the imagination, unbased on personal experience, [Crane's] realism would be nothing short of a miracle." But Crane, born in 1871, had not been to the war and in an important sense was not a Realist, did not present what he had seen, with fidelity, the way he had seen it. Indeed, in terms of sharpness of detail, his stories of war written after he had seen battle in Cuba and Greece are inferior to the earlier ones which were purely imaginative. Nor was Crane a Naturalist, tracing the causal history of the effects of Deterministic forces in the lives of his characters. Rather, Crane's gifts were those of a creative imagination which could represent, in detail, the sensational nature of human experience. In the creation of the illusion of sensory reality, Stephen Crane had no equals in his time.

The limitation of narrative data in fiction to the narrator's projection of the mind of a character is central to Impressionism, as is the suggestion that the perceiving intelligence is a qualification of the definition of reality, that perceptions are relative and potentially unreliable, that interpretations of reality are forever tentative, and that other minds may perceive the same phenomenon in other terms. One extension of this logic leads to narrative modulations of shifting perspectives, of multiple, sometimes reduplicative presentations of scenes in narrative parallax; another would lead to narrative irony, to the concentration not only on sensory data but on the way it is perceived at either the apprehensional or comprehensional level. For example, in *The Red Badge of Courage* the narrator at one point records Henry Fleming's view of horses and riders in the distance without correction for spatial reduction. The sensory data is that "once he [Henry] saw a tiny battery go dashing along the line of the horizon. The tiny riders were beating the tiny horses." In similar fashion, in the opening paragraph of "The Bride Comes to Yellow Sky" the narrator can assert, as the train whirls westward carrying Jack Potter and his bride, that "the plains of Texas were pouring eastward. Vast flats of green grass, dull-hued spaces of mesquite and cactus, little groups of frame houses, woods of light and tender trees, all were sweeping over the horizon, a precipice."

It is also possible for the narrator to present comprehensional error, judgmental activity, as in *The Red Badge* when the lieutenant admonishes Henry to keep within ranks: "He mended his pace with suitable haste. And he hated the lieutenant, who had no appreciation of fine minds. He was a mere brute." The irony, of course, results from Henry's self-revelation and from the inevitable awareness for the reader that the problem is not so much the lieutenant's brutishness as Henry's grandiose view of his own "fine mind." The central narrative method of *The Red Badge* is thus a continuous pattern of ironic presentations of distorted judgments by Henry rendered faithfully by the narrator, a method which reveals how Henry's mind, driven by fear and doubt and shame, reconstructs the data of reality to create a context in which his own actions can be seen in a positive, often an heroic, light. So it is in *Maggie* that the narrator can assert, without qualification, that Pete "was a knight," an "aristocratic person," by projecting Maggie's judgments, and in *George's Mother* state that Mrs. Kelcey "was a perfect mother, rearing a perfect son," revealing her simplistic perception of what is left of her family.

The theoretical logic of Impressionism thus tends toward variations of limited narrative perspectives. First-person narration is attractive here, but problematic: it contains the virtue of spatial immediacy but the enigma of temporal dislocation. In nearly all of its expressions it implies a dual time scheme, a time of telling subsequent to the time of action; the narrator thus renders memory rather than sensory experience. As a basically Impressionistic writer, Crane had difficulty with this mode and used it infrequently and in none of his finest works. His few first-person works, however, reveal fascinating manipulations of perspective which bring them into greater conformity with Impressionistic concepts. "A Tale of Mere Chance," for example, is a dramatic monologue which presents the ironic revelations of a murderer telling his story after his capture. What the story reveals is that his judgment of himself is inconsistent with the very facts he presents: he has shot a man point-blank and without warning yet attempts to maintain his view of himself as a "delicate and sensitive person." The story portrays his pervasive guilt and the interpretive aberrations of his mind, as is especially evident in his surrealistic personification of inanimate objects. According to *his* version of it, when he attempted to escape the scene of the murder, the chair moved to block the door; the clock speaks to betray his alibi; his blood-stained coat clings to him; the floor tiles, stained by blood, pursue him, relentlessly "shrieking" his guilt. The story is first person, but more suggestive of Impressionistic distortion than of traditional uses of the method. Another example is "An Illusion in Red and White," in which the narrator can only speculate about what happened and in which the children, eyewitnesses to the murder of their mother, delude themselves completely by the end of the story. The result of Crane's handling of first person is to introduce unreliability and irony as important modifiers of the plot, a device Ford Madox Ford used with success in *The Good Soldier.*

Another traditional narrative device theoretically problematic for Impressionism is third-person omniscient, since, by the logic of its own assumptions, it is not dependent upon the empirical data of the fiction for its information. Only a few of Crane's works are truly consistent with the terms of omniscience, and these are among his least impressive works. *The Third Violet* and *Active Service,* two of what Lillian Gilkes has called Crane's "potboiler" novels, are basically omniscient in that the narrator roams freely in space and time with access to the minds of all the characters. But beyond these two novels, there is little of traditional omniscience in Crane's works except in such minor pieces as "Henry M. Stanley" which is notable only for being one of the works by Crane entirely free of irony.

If first-person narration is temporally awkward for Impressionism, and omniscience philosophically discordant, its natural expression is third-person limited, the mode Crane almost consistently used, although with numerous variations. Crane's method is basically focused on the sensory and associational experience of the central character. His style is thus understandably laden with verbs of perception. Sergio Perosa's study of *The Red Badge,* which he describes as a "triumph of impressionistic vision and impressionistic technique," reveals 350 verbs directly indicating vision, another 250 verbs, such as "appear," which suggest visual phenomena, and numerous auditory and tactile images. Perosa's point is to emphasize the extent to which the novel is a record of Henry's sensory experiences.

But an even more emphatic example of Crane's Impressionistic strategies is the presentation of sensory data under extraordinary circumstances of restriction. He relates one such moment in his "London Impressions" in describing the experiences of a carriage ride: "Each man sat in his own little cylinder of vision, so to speak. It was not so small as a sentry-box, nor so large as a circus-tent, but the walls were opaque, and what was passing beyond the dimensions of his cylinder no man knew." The "cylinder of vision" concept, which Milne Holton used for the title of his impressive book, is a useful metaphor for the implicit human condition in all of Crane's work and a suggestive indicator of his manner of narration. Perhaps the most dramatic brief demonstration of this method is in a little-studied story entitled "Three Miraculous Soldiers," in which the point of view is essentially restricted to the mind of its female protagonist, Mary Hickson, who gains much of her information, especially at the most suspenseful moments, by peering through a knothole into a dimly lit barn.

The opening of the story reveals Crane's typical method of progressive intensification: the first paragraph describes Mary and the room she is in from the outside perspective of a third-person narrator: "The girl was in the front room on the second floor, peering through the blinds." The point of view is outside of Mary and yet is not omniscient: the narrator must speculate that the two clay figures on the mantel are "probably" a shepherd and shepherdess. Beyond introducing a characteristic uncertainty, the opening paragraph also defines Mary's initial angle of vision which then controls the second paragraph: "from between the slats of the blinds she had a view of the road as it wended across the meadow to the woods and again where it reappeared crossing the hill, a half mile away." Now there are no comments beyond Mary's knowledge; implied, but not stated, is the suggestion that she is deeply concerned with the activity on the road, of which she can see only part. By the third paragraph the narrative perspective is limited to Mary's mind and her sensory information:

> Mary's eyes were fastened upon the little streak of road that appeared on the distant hill. Her face was flushed with excitement and the hand which stretched in a strained pose on the sill trembled because of the nervous shaking of the wrist. The pines whisked their green needles with a soft hissing sound against the house.

The story progresses on these limited terms. When Mary speaks to someone downstairs, "a voice" answers. Not until further dialogue establishes the identity of the voice does the narrator clarify that it is that of the mother. This method is similar to that in *The Red Badge,* in which speakers are identified only by descriptive epithets until personal names have been mentioned in dialogue. When the soldiers first appear on the road, they do so at a distance, a fact rendered Impressionistically: "Upon the yellow streak of road that lay across the hillside there now was a handful of black dots—horsemen." It is indicative of Crane's method of presenting apprehension before cognition that he does not say that "soldiers" appeared in the distance. Mary's eyes perceive "black dots" which are then interpreted as horsemen, the next level of analysis, and finally as soldiers, as opposed to other categories of horsemen.

To Mary's point of view is added another, one equally limited: "Rushing to the window, the mother scanned for an instant the road on the hill." The mother responds with fright, apparently from what the soldiers might do, but it is clear that they are still at some distance, for in a moment "the black dots vanished into the wood." Soon the girl can hear the "quick, dull trample of horses." When they appear, the forest suddenly "disclosing" them in their blue uniforms, the fictional situation is further clarified: this is a house in the South; Mary and her family are loyal Confederates; the Union army is advancing. The perspective briefly shifts to that of the officer in charge of the group, revealing his lack of interest in the house and its inhabitants. His insouciance becomes significant when set against the counteranalysis of his motives by the mother, who is convinced that the ruthless Yankees are about to take advantage of two defenseless women. Emotional preoccupation, in subjective Impressionistic terms, serves to distort the interpretation of sensory data. As a result, the women hear the crackling of the fire in the kitchen as the movement of soldiers: "These sounds were sinister." Apprehensive data has now become mingled with interpretive distortions on the secondary level of Impressionistic information. The first section of the story ends when Mary goes to the barn to relieve her fears that her horse has been stolen and discovers three Confederate soldiers hiding from the Union advance. Again, the narrative emphasis is on restriction: at first "the girl could not see into the barn because of the heavy shadows." In a moment, when her eyes adjust to the light, her perception is of "three men in gray" sitting on the floor. That the men are Confederate soldiers in hiding is left to the reader to induce.

The next section of the story retains its restriction on the point of view to Mary's mind and what she is able to see. As she speaks to the soldiers, seeking information about her father, and as a large group of Union cavalry ride into the yard, the emphasis is on how little Mary can see and understand of the events. The trees and a henhouse obscure her view of the arriving troops; she has to leave the barn to get a better look at them; once in the house, she moves about from window to window, each revealing only a partial view of the scene. No clarifying information is introduced here from any source other than Mary's mind. By the end of the section she has hidden the three men in the feed box in the barn and the Union soldiers have decided to imprison a captured Confederate there as well, not knowing of the presence of the others.

The next section becomes increasingly vivid in its projection of sensory details as the scene becomes obscure and limited. As it begins to grow dark, Mary, back in the house peering out the window, perceives the muted colors before her: "Tones of grey came upon the fields and the shadows were of lead." The fires in the encampment shine more brilliantly, "becoming spots of crimson color in the dark grove." As the light fades even further, visual data becomes more indistinct: trees become black "streaks of ink"; groups of soldiers become "blue clouds" about the fire. A lantern hung in the barn distorts the view:

"Its rays made the form of the sentry seem gigantic." Auditory sensation, understandably, is not affected: the whinny of the horses, the "hum" of distant conversation, the calls of the sentries are all received clearly. That all of this is Impressionistic in broad terms is further suggested by Mary's assessment of the scene in the orchard, with campfires glowing in the darkness, as one "like a great painting, all in reds upon a black cloth." Finally, in the ultimate restriction of narrative data, Mary, stealing to the rear of the barn to confirm the safety of her compatriots in the feed box, puts her eye to a knothole. Much of the rest of the story is rendered from this perspective.

There is a tense scene when a Union officer opens the feed box and finds nothing but grain. Having no access to data beyond her own experience, Mary is startled and mystified. Incapable of accounting for the disappearance of the three men, Mary's mind perceives the feed box as a mysterious object "like some dark magician's trap." Through the knothole, the Union soldiers cast "monstrous wavering shadows" in the lantern light; the roof of the barn becomes an "inscrutable blackness." Her mind becomes incapable of interpreting sensory data reliably: hearing sounds at her feet, she first "imagines" that she sees human hands protruding from under the barn; then she realizes that they are, in fact, hands; then she sees a man crawling out. Despite the dramatic circumstances, there is more stress on Mary's problems of perception and interpretation than on suspenseful activity. The three Confederates escape from the barn only to learn that their captain is still being held within. They decide to attempt to rescue him.

As the soldiers return to the barn, Mary resumes her vigil at the knothole, and what is revealed about the ensuing action is limited to what she can perceive from this vantage point. When she first looks about the area, "she searched with her eyes, trying to detect some moving thing, but she could see nothing." She thinks she can see a figure moving in the darkness, but she is not sure: "At one time she saw it plainly and at other times it vanished, because her fixture of gaze caused her occasionally to greatly tangle and blur those peculiar shadows and faint lights. At last, however, she perceived a human head." Her other perceptions are equally difficult. The sounds of activity which come to her are incomprehensible: she can interpret them only in general terms as a "tumult," as the "scramble and scamper of feet," as voices yelling "incoherent" words. As the sentry moves into her vision, however, and as her sense of his danger from the creeping men within the barn grows, she focuses sharply on his "brown hair," "clear eyes," and on the ring on his finger signifying marriage. When the men finally leap upon the sentry, Mary's passive reception of details ends and she screams, inadvertently creating a diversion which allows the four Confederates to escape. The story ends with the Union lieutenant reflecting on Mary's concern for the sentry, an indication that despite war some elements of universal human compassion survive.

"Three Miraculous Soldiers" is no more a real story of war than is *The Red Badge.* The story is perhaps Crane's best use of suspense in the narrative line, but even the suspense is a product of the narrative method. Told from an omniscient point of view, there could have been little suspenseful interest. The story is artistically and ideologically a study in the limitations of sensory data, rendered, with some contrasts from other limited viewpoints, from the mind of Mary Hickson under conditions of extraordinary restriction. Although there are other elements of interest (the depiction of war from the point of view of a southern woman; melodramatic plot developments; a concern for the father off at war), the fundamental themes and methods of this story are Impressionistic. Indeed, the lengthy scenes told on the basis of what Mary can perceive through the knothole constitute one of the most remarkably limited narrative perspectives in American literature.

A few of Crane's other methods of narration, all coordinate with central Impressionistic implications, deserve comment. One such device is the "camera eye" technique used in the fight scene in "The Blue Hotel" when the perspective becomes that of the Easterner: "During this pause, the Easterner's mind, like a film, took lasting impressions of three men—the iron-nerved master of the ceremony; the Swede, pale, motionless, terrible; and Johnnie, serene yet ferocious, brutish yet heroic." Limited to the vision of the Easterner, a small man, fraught with anxiety, peering into a snowstorm, the narrator can record only fragmentary glimpses: "For a time the encounter in the darkness was such a perplexity of flying arms that it presented no more detail than would a swiftly-revolving wheel. Occasionally a face, as if illuminated by a flash of light, would shine out, ghastly and marked with pink spots." This scene is similar to one in "A Man and Some Others" in which another Easterner observes a gunfight at night between Bill and a band of Mexicans attempting to run him off the range: "The lightning action of the next few moments was of the fabric of dreams to the stranger. . . . And so the fight, and his part in it, had to the stranger only the quality of a picture half drawn."

An especially noteworthy narrative device used by Crane is "parallax," the device of narrating from more than one point of view, usually two or more limited perspectives, occasionally limited views set off against an omniscient narrator. Crane used this method throughout his life, from "Uncle Jake and the Bell-Handle," a story written when he was only fourteen, and in which the rustic Uncle Jake's perspective is comically juxtaposed to that of the worldly-wise urban clerks, to similar devices in "The Bride Comes to Yellow Sky" and "The Open Boat," to perhaps his most notable implementation of the method in "Death and the Child." In this story Peza's view of war as an heroic struggle is counterpointed by the view of the child, who sees it as an extension of his game of shepherding. The contrasting points of view in such works reinforce the notion of relativity, that phenomenological perception is as important in understanding reality as the external objects themselves. And it is historically important to remember that Crane's use of parallax is antecedent to Ernest Hemingway's use of it in "The Short Happy Life of Francis Macomber" and William Faulkner's more sophisticated implementation in *The Sound and the Fury* and *As I Lay Dying*.

To make a simple statement about an extremely intricate matter, Stephen Crane's narrative methods are a good deal more complex than has generally been assumed, especially by those readers who would simply identify the narrators of his works as Crane himself. His narrative methods, almost without exception, portray a world which is "ephemeral, evanescent, constantly shifting its meaning and hence continually defying precise definition," a description Rodney O. Rogers uses to describe both Crane's works and French Impressionistic painting. Narrative restrictions, limitations of sensory data, distorted interpretations of information, modulations among differing points of view, these are Crane's methods of presentation. As a more complete analysis of Crane's works would reveal, these narrative strategies are related to his episodic plots, his sensory images, his epistemological themes involving perception and realization. As a totality, Crane's works suggest a human situation in which the individual is almost inconsequential in the universal matrix and yet is a dramatic modifier of all of reality he can ever know, a situation in which any view of circumstances is limited, philosophically tentative, and certain to be challenged by contrasting views. It is an unsettling yet aesthetically satisfying conception, one remarkably modern and existential for the 1890s, one basic to what has been called Crane's "vision," and one central to the fundamental implications of literary Impressionism.

HAROLD KAPLAN

Vitalism and Redemptive Violence

The naturalist obsession with violence can, when conditioned by an imaginative sensibility and raised to the level of revelation—emerge in the form of ritual observations and ceremonial drama. Stephen Crane had that kind of sensibility, tightening what is loose allegory in Norris, and in *The Red Badge of Courage* he developed a poetry of violence that singles that book out in the mainstream of naturalist fiction.

Crane did not need to know the Civil War personally because he knew it so well imaginatively; all that he needed were the naturalist myths that fed his imagination. His book is powerful, standing out above the works of Norris, London, and even Dreiser, not because it documents the life of camp and battle but because it is highly focused on primitive mysteries in battle and death.

Crane is clearly attempting to give a religious coloring to these revelations. Nature contains a god, and his service is sacrifice and death. War is nature's stormy Mount Sinai, "war, the red animal—war, the blood-swollen god." All that nature contains of great force, pain, death, extreme physical effort, and ultimate physical collapse are given their high ground of revelation in war. It is there that these naturalist truths meet and converge on a metaphysical level. And when Henry Fleming is most absorbed by the battle, he knows war in this way: "He himself felt the daring spirit of a savage, religion—mad. He was capable of profound sacrifices, a tremendous death."

But since Henry is entirely oblivious of the political or moral justifications of this war, his battle crisis reveals only the cosmic processes of survival

From *Power and Order: Henry Adams and the Naturalist Tradition in American Fiction.* © 1981 by The University of Chicago. University of Chicago Press, 1981.

and death. Here can be found naturalism's nearest approach to religious transcendence, and it occurs at the boundaries of biological fate. And this is the essence of naturalist heroism: to approach the mystery of nature depends on the will to confront its most savage truth, sacrificing a mundane safety. Crane mentions "profound sacrifices," but it is clear that these sacrifices have no specific moral purpose. The value is metaphysical and personal, and the antagonist is not a human being but natural violence and death.

Violence possesses awesome meaning here because it opens toward death. The major confrontation with naturalist mystery is not in battle itself, for it comes to Henry Fleming when he is running away from battle. The scene is described in explicitly religious terms:

> He reached a place where the high, arching boughs made a chapel.
> He softly pushed the green doors aside and entered. Pine needles
> were a gentle brown carpet. There was a religious half light.
>   Near the threshold he stopped, horror-stricken at the sight of
> a thing.

The "thing" is a dead man, seated with his back against a tree, and the chapel containing that thing expresses the lucid power of Crane's imagination. Crane of course complicates the religious references with the irony that is characteristic of all his writing, but here the irony is complex, not obviously reductive. Nothing of the shock of physical death is withheld; the eyes of the dead man have "the dull hue to be seen on the side of a dead fish," and

> Over the grey skin of the face ran little ants. One was trundling
> some sort of bundle along the upper lip.

In the midst of all this horror, "The dead man and the living man exchanged a long look." Then the scene draws softly to a close, as if it had brought spiritual comfort.

> The trees about the portals of the chapel moved soughingly in a
> soft wind. A sad silence was upon the little guarding edifice.

A fuller initiation into the mystery of death takes place later, in the prolonged agony of Henry's friend, Jim Conklin. As he walks beside Henry in the parade of the wounded, Jim is dying on his feet, staring into the unknown: "he seemed always looking for a place, like one who goes to choose a grave," and, already spectral in his look, he says, "don't tech me—leave me be." The dying man is preparing himself: "there was something ritelike in these movements of the doomed soldier." When the place and the moment are finally reached, there is an effect of ennoblement and transfiguration: "He was at the rendezvous . . . there was a curious and profound dignity in the firm lines of his awful face."

The dignity might reflect natural process: Conklin's last moment is like the falling of a tree, "a slight rending sound." But, with his mouth open, "the teeth showed in a laugh." The laugh dismisses a sentimental primitivism, and Conklin, when he falls, reveals the side of his body, which looks "as if it had been chewed by wolves." Fleming at this moment shakes his fist at the battlefield, getting out only one word, "Hell—." Following this is a line that has stirred debate among various critics as to its serious or ironic implication: "The red sun was pasted in the sky like a wafer." Given the context, it would seem absurd to miss the irony of this reference to Christlike dying and to the Communion. Still, if Crane is here employing his characteristic irony, he is at the same time confirming the universal ritual modes for confronting the experience of death.

The allusion to Christ emphasizes the vulnerability of the religious imagination, a pathos that is frequent in naturalist writing. Here irony and pathos come together in the seeming laugh of the dying man, enforcing his stoic dignity. He dies as a tree falls, and he has chosen his place to die after walking for a long time with a horrible wound in his side. There is not only a natural mystery here but a moral lesson. Conklin himself has no doubt transcended the motivation of pride in his personal bearing, but Fleming seems to have learned something from it, and this is related to the ostensible theme of Crane's book, the "red badge" of an initiation into courage. Just as the mystery religions of nature reached their deepest revelations in death, so here a specifically naturalist ethic is death-oriented. Almost immediately after Conklin's death, which might have confirmed him more than ever in his desire to run away, Henry begins to envision, instead, a return to his comrades, among whom, restored to self-respect by leading a charge in battle, he sees himself "getting calmly killed before the eyes of all. . . . He thought of the magnificent pathos of his dead body."

The awe and fierce dignity of Conklin's death confirmed that "magnificent pathos." It is a death-pathos now linked to the spirit of "a savage religion" requiring "profound sacrifices." The forest chapel of death, where ants trailed over the dead soldier's lips, affirmed the harsh terms of a soldier's religion, and further, and conclusive, emphasis is placed on Henry's redemptive initiation in battle: "He had been to touch the great death, and found that, after all, it was but the great death. He was a man." The values of this manhood are vitalist, and Crane views their implications with detachment: "He had been where there was red of blood and black of passion, and he was escaped. . . . He saw that he was good." Did the "good" reside in Henry's escape or in his authentication by blood and passion? At that margin of experience it is not possible to distinguish between survival and authenticity, or self-realization.

Critics have argued about this conclusion of Crane's story. Some have accepted Fleming's apotheosis in courage, while others continue to challenge the notion that Crane was seriously attempting to define a code of virile honor. I doubt, myself, that Crane was capable of writing a line describing subjective human commitments without leaving the door open for implicit irony. He was that kind of naturalist—indeed, in his uncorrupted detachment he resembles Flaubert or Joyce—and it is from that perspective, with a lucidity that is almost inevitably ironic, that he viewed the male-oriented vitalism of hunting, fighting, and survival. In this he presents a precise contrast with Adams's cult of the Virgin. Yet it might seem that, moved by the same intellectual needs as Adams, Crane was led to a parallel sexual vitalism but one almost inevitably "machoist" in tendency (later to be elaborated in the works of Hemingway and Norman Mailer).

The naturalist ethic in which the red of blood and the black of passion are the banner of manhood and lead the way to the "good" finds easy reinforcement in the group. The battle ordeal and the natural laws of pain and death set the conditions for the "subtle battle brotherhood" of the men who fight together. In the end, after both loss and victory, the regiment has become "a mysterious fraternity born of the smoke and danger of death." The brotherhood of soldiers expresses the force of the vitalist cult as it might be applied to nations, races, and classes. These are collectivities committed to historic conflict and survival. Promoting the ethic of conflict, they learn to translate danger into fraternity; perhaps they even invite violence in order to learn fraternity.

In Crane's completely clear view of this theme, the only suffering that exceeds physical suffering, and could make the latter welcome, is that of the moral outcast. Similarly, the only emotion that can compete with fear is shame. After Henry Fleming has run from battle, his fear lessens and he is gradually possessed by the self-ostracism of the moral refugee. As he walks among the wounded, he encounters the "tattered man," and the latter's desire to compare wounds probes into his cowardice. "The simple questions of the tattered man had been knife thrusts to him. They asserted a society." What Henry needs now is a wound of his own, and he longs for it, his "red badge of courage." The blow he receives from another fleeing soldier gives him what he wants, and he is able to return to his regiment. The wound is unworthy, but the link between its sign and his self-respect has been emphasized. Now he has the chance to redeem himself in another battle, and he does.

The power of emulation thus matches the power of pain and death. It is perhaps this equation in naturalist thought that is the key to some of its deepest political implications. Nature's force and process are absorbed and dominated by the social process, but this in turn is ruled by natural law. In an army the reasons for valuing courage and the ability to endure pain and face death are obvious. Nevertheless, Crane's description of the army as a social unit and a moral force establish it as something much greater than an instrument for winning wars. His imagery is, as usual, concise and telling: "It [the regiment] inclosed him. And there were iron laws of tradition and law on four sides. He was in a moving box." The army as a thing, a box, alternates with images of the army as a serpent, a dragon, a monster. The interesting question is how this imagery supports rather than undercuts the army's function as a disciplined moral instrument, capable of collective judgment: "The regiment was like a firework," Crane writes, a thing ready to explode with its force. The point is actually to eliminate a traditional concept of judgment. This collectivity, enforcing behavior, is viewed as power in itself in its ability to evoke emulation, fear, shame, and pride.

The "naturalness" of this power is emphasized by the clarity with which Crane saw that to bring up the cause for fighting would have no relevance. There is no war here in the ordinary political and geographic sense. There are two armies, but they are distinguished only by the color of their uniforms. And the generals, who think they have control over the battle, actually do not. They send only inconsistent and incomprehensible orders, and they preside over actual confusion: for, whether running away or running forward, "the running men . . . were all deaf and blind."

Accordingly, when the group power of the army is not a prisonlike enclosure of tradition and law, it becomes simply a "floodlike force." Either way, the species dominates, absorbs, and transcends individual instincts and all personal interests, including survival itself. The group is not led but driven, both from within and from without; it either compulsively obeys tradition or anarchically surrenders to chaos. The army as a mob is as definite a force as the army under discipline. Nothing really distinguishes this society from simple organic or mechanical force except the spirit of emulation. If the approach of battle reveals to Henry that "he knew nothing of himself" and that "he was an unknown quantity," it also reveals that there is not much to know beyond the realities of fear and courage, strength and weakness. For the rest, "he continually tried to measure himself by his comrades" ; it was their good opinion he wanted. Henry's mind is at times filled with conventional battle romanticism, with notions of breathless deeds observed by "heavy crowns and high castles," but this traditional idealization of war is treated as a thin layer of childlike fantasy superimposed on more basic forces: the "moving box" of the army and the "throat-grappling" instinct for battle.

Still, as I have noted, these more basic forces are themselves the source of idealizations, of purely naturalist values. One is the vitalist virtue of proven manhood, of macho courage. Another is Henry's feeling of sublimity in the presence of "tremendous death" or in "the magnificent pathos of his [own] dead body." This might be called the moral code of Thanatos, calling for "an enthusiasm of unselfishness," "a sublime recklessness . . . shattered against the iron gates of the impossible." The highest virtue learned in naturalist conflict thus seems to be self-immolation. Behind war, "the blood-swollen god," stands death, a greater god, and the question that needs review is the extent to which the naturalist myth finds itself in service to the gods of *greatest* strength. The death pathos has no rival in its power to stir human emotions; recognizing this, Crane went further than most naturalist writers in appreciating the primitive compulsions of attraction and dread that death exerts.

Let us then trace the clear outline of Crane's naturalist values. Primordial violence, "the red animal," releases the most elemental and unsocialized passions and instincts. But since in Crane's work this occurs in the context of opposed armies, it results in elemental socialization. Henry Fleming's only defense against the fear of death, and perhaps against the attractions of death, is the approval of his comrades. He knew his greatest despair when he was alone, isolated from the rest of the army. Confronting death, he comes back to the army and experiences great relief, as if here was the only alternative to metaphysical panic. Social membership is almost as absolute as death, and it receives from death a kind of existential sanction, giving to Henry all the confidence of being that he can have. In all of this the crisis of violence is indispensable, for it proves the need for high group discipline and, in a naturalist paradox, juxtaposes primitive savagery with highly organized behavior. The battle scene brings together the reality of power and conflict and a primitive social ethic at its point of inception. In fact, if one wonders why the ethos of naturalist political movements, whether fascist or communist, is imbued with authoritarian discipline, the most direct answer would be that, in assuming the universality of group conflict as the premise for their existence, they needed to organize and motivate themselves like armies.

REDEMPTIVE VIOLENCE

In *The Red Badge of Courage,* a novel of war, where the opportunity to expose social illusions and oppressions was most available, Crane chose to concentrate on primitive collective psychology and instinctual experience.

He pointedly avoids the social and historical issues of the Civil War. The deepest reading of Crane, I myself believe, emphasizes a tragic naturalism or a pessimism directed at both natural violence and social rule. But it is arguable, to a degree limited somewhat by his ironic sensibility, that Crane, in both *Maggie* and *The Red Badge of Courage,* is a vitalist in whom high respect for truth fuses with stoic faith in nature. Certainly he traces the growth of a neoprimitive, stoic religion of nature in his characters, as in Henry Fleming's inchoate respect for the gods of death and war. Essential to it is the ordeal, the arena in which the hero finds value in pain, violence, and even death— accepts them as productive of good. The ethos that naturalism develops is thus based on the struggle for survival, and it features that combination of sacrificial and stoic virtues described by Lovejoy as "hard primitivism." Nietzsche was the modern teacher of these stoic values when he said, in making his own great claim to naturalist revelations, that he would rather perish than renounce the truth that "life sacrifices itself—for the sake of power!" The various forms of redemptive or cathartic violence expressed in the works of Crane and Hemingway and by many later disciples, in both fiction and film, are specifically Nietzschean motifs in the modern myth of power.

CAROL HURD GREEN

Stephen Crane and the Fallen Women

Stephen Crane, who died at twenty-eight, was always a young writer. Nowhere is his youth more apparent than in his attitude toward women. In a letter to an early love, Nellie Crouse, he wrote of himself:

> So you think I am successful? Well I don't know. Most people consider me successful. At least, they seem to so think. But upon my soul I have lost all appetite for victory, as victory is defined by the mob. I will be glad if I can feel on my death-bed that my life has been just and kind according to my ability and that every particle of my little ridiculous stock of eloquence and wisdom has been applied for the benefit of my kind. From this moment to that death-bed may be a short time or a long one but at any rate it means a life of labor and sorrow. I do not confront it blithely. I confront it with desperate resolution. . . . I do not expect to do good. But I expect to make a sincere, desperate, lonely battle to remain true to my conception of my life. . . . It is not a fine prospect. I only speak of it to people in whose opinions I have faith. No woman has heard it until now.

The tone is stylishly world-weary, the voice that of an eager, appealing, and literary self-absorbed youth whose infatuation with himself is clear. He professes himself infatuated as well with Nellie, but the measure of his regard is in the assurance that she is worthy of his confidence.

In Crane's poetry and fiction, such self-absorption and high intentions

From *American Novelists Revisited: Essays in Feminist Criticism,* edited by Fritz Fleischmann. © 1982 by Fritz Fleischmann. G. K. Hall, 1982.

leave women out of serious consideration; they are never more than images. And the images are those seen from a perspective of adolescence: women are mothers or crabby-teacher figures or gossips, sexless and shapeless, manufacturing and exerting authority, or—if they are young and shapely—seductresses, or (like Grace Fanhall in *The Third Violet*) the stuff of which romantic dreams are made. In the presence of women, men are driven to nonsense, silence, impotence, or guilt. Women, too, fall prey to members of their own sex; there is not among them the loyalty of brotherhood that Crane, the "preacher's kid," created as a faith. It was that capacity for loyalty that redeemed men; without it, all women—not just the prostitutes who fascinated Crane—were fallen women.

Some could be rescued, if the man was sufficiently intrepid and the woman suitable for rescuing. It is not new to point to the recurrence in Crane of the rescue motif. In 1950, John Berryman set out to explain the pattern of Crane's relationships with women. He noted the writer's attraction to older, often unattainable, and sometimes morally dubious women and his continuous fascination with prostitutes, culminating in his common-law marriage to Cora Stewart, proprietor of the Hotel de Dream, a brothel in Jacksonville, Florida. Berryman offered a Freudian explanation, seeing Crane as an example of the man described in Freud's "A Special Type of Choice of Objects Made by Men" (1910). Such a person seeks a woman in whom another man has some "right of possession," and/or one who is to some extent "sexually discredited" and whose "fidelity and loyalty" are open to doubt. The lover, intense and sincere, will manifest, in his compulsion to repeat such relationships, a desire to rescue the woman.

Daniel Hoffman, in his book on Crane's poetry, agreed. He saw Crane's attachment for his early loves—Helen Trent, Nellie Crouse, Lily Brandon Munroe—as well as for a number of demimonde figures as confirmation of Berryman's analysis, and also emphasized Crane's wish to rescue them from "plights sometimes imaginary." For Hoffman, however, the explanation of Crane's behavior was not to be found solely in psychology, but also in religion. Crane's "mode of interpreting experience" can be seen as deeply influenced by his Methodist heritage. In Hoffman's view, this heritage created in the young author a profound moral anxiety about sexual love, leading him to believe that "to love is to be damned." Further, Hoffman points out, in Crane's poetry the blame for this damnation is consistently placed on the woman; she is the aggressor and seductress, he is the victim.

Like the fiction, Crane's poetry pays relatively little attention to women; Crane's imagination functions best in the world of men. When the poetry does concentrate on women, it reveals a simultaneous fascination with and revulsion from female sexuality, and a mingling of images of nineties' decadence with the petulance of a failed lover. Three poems are especially relevant here: the series of verses titled "Intrigue" from the *War Is Kind* volume, the poem from the same collection that begins "On the desert," and the updated brief verse, "A naked woman and a dead dwarf." "Intrigue" provides the most direct illustration of Hoffman's point about the transference of blame: the handwringing anguish and the accusations of infidelity swirl and spit out among verses of sentimental exaggeration.

> Thou art my love
> And thou art a weary violet
> Drooping from sun-caresses.
> Answering mine carelessly
> Woe is me.
> . . . .
> Thou art my love
> And thou art the ashes of other men's love
> And I bury my face in these ashes
> And I love them
> Woe is me.
> . . . .
> Thou art my love
> And thou art a priestess
> And in thy hand is a bloody dagger
> And my doom comes to me surely
> Woe is me.

The images are self-absorbed and angry. They sink to bathos— "I weep and I gnash / And I love the little shoe / The little, little shoe" —and seldom rise beyond self-pity. The theme is struck here, as it will be frequently throughout Crane's work: women, being incapable of fidelity, make men into fools. Being without honesty, they make mockery of men's attempts to transcend human limits. Like the "little man" who inhabits so much of Crane's fiction, the lover is reduced to posturing and pomposity:

> God give me loud honors
> That I may strut before you, sweetheart
> And be worthy of—
> —The love I bear you

to fantasies of brutality:

And I wish to be an ogre
And hale and haul my beloved to a castle
And there use the happy cruel one cruelly
And make her mourn with my mourning

and of chivalry

I have heard your quick breaths
And seen your arms writhe toward me;
At those times
—God help us—
I was impelled to be a grand knight.

But that, too, leads to self-mockery: the knight would "Swagger and snap my fingers, / And explain my mind finely."

The woman here, as in "On the desert," is like a snake: her arms "writhe" toward her lover. The echo of the Garden of Eden, the tempting snake, is combined with the popular nineties image of the sinuous Salomé in the shorter poem. "On the desert" is a silent movie of the seductress and her victims, the "squat and dumb" men who are hypnotized into powerlessness by her. Sinister and deadly, she and the snakes work their will:

[S]low things, sinuous, dull with terrible color
Sleepily fondle her body
Or move at her will, . . .
And over the sand serpents move warily
Slow, menacing and submissive,
. . . .
But always whispering, softly whispering.
The dignity of the accurséd;
The glory of slavery, despair, death
Is in the dance of the whispering snakes.

Caught in her trap, the men have left only paradox—the glory of the fall, of slavery, despair, and death, a romantic, self-destructive bondage to sex, to woman.

The risk of being made a fool of, of being false to oneself, dominates Crane's view of men's fate in the presence of women. In "A naked woman and a dead dwarf" he strips both parties to the essentials. The man is the fool in cap and bells, truly the little man, the dwarf—and perhaps a more exact figure of impotence—and the woman is naked.

A naked woman and a dead dwarf;

Wealth and indifference.
Poor dwarf!
Reigning with foolish kings
And dying mid bells and wine
Ending with a desperate and comic palaver
While before thee and after thee
Endures the eternal clown—
—The eternal clown—
A naked woman.

Here the little man is clearly identified with the artist. "Ending with a desperate comic palaver," he endures the final humiliation. The woman survives.

The temptation to autobiographical readings of Crane's portraits of women is strong. But it is less fruitful to see this poem as simply Crane being angry in advance at his wife for outliving him than to see it within the context of the destructive tension between honesty and dishonesty, morality and immorality, the making of art and its destruction, that Crane sees as the relation between man and woman. In that relation, man and especially man as artist (there are no creative women in Crane) is driven into posturing and fantasy or forced into silence and self-betrayal.

The experiment in form that his poems represented apparently freed Crane to express the deeper associations of ideas and emotions that governed his imagination—bitterness, irony, and anger as well as a high romantic self-image are all more openly expressed. The fiction was a different matter: the stories were written to attract a large reading public and to earn him a living. There were forms ready to hand—the tract, the adventure story, the small-town tale—and he turned to them, while transforming each to suit his purposes. In so doing, Crane modified his portrayal of women but did not turn away from his conviction that they were the troublemakers, noisy, disloyal, and destructive.

Only passive women, those who could be rescued by men and be properly grateful for it, like Marjory Wainwright in *Active Service* (1899) or the bride who came to Yellow Sky, were exceptions. They allowed men to find and express their better selves: the married Jack Potter, Sheriff of Yellow Sky, defeats Scratchy Wilson once and for all, and without violence. His bride, "not pretty, nor . . . very young," the bearer of a "plain, under-class countenance," and rescued by Potter from the drudgery of being someone's cook, looks on. Rufus Coleman, the sophisticated, hard-drinking editor of the Sunday edition of the yellow *New York Eclipse,* rushes off to save Marjory and her parents from a terrible fate in the midst of the Greco-Turkish war. She, well trained in the modesty becoming a lady, maintains her dignity and transforms him into a figure of innocent happiness; *Active Service* ends in a romantic fade-out clearly designed to please the serial-reading audience for whom, in the rush of trying to finish the novel and pay his bills, Crane in the end designed the book.

Active Service was originally to be a "big book" about the Greco-Turkish war, benefiting from Crane's experience as a war correspondent. But between 1897, when he began the book, and 1899, when, in failing health, he hurried to complete it, the focus changed. The war becomes a faint backdrop to a tale of chivalry and of the war between the sexes. Coleman is in love with Marjory, whose professor father takes her to Greece to get her away from her unsuitable suitor, only to plunge her, his wife, and the students he brought along into danger. Coleman, dashing off to the rescue, encounters on shipboard Nora Black, the "queen of comic opera," who then throws up her London theatrical engagement to pursue Coleman and add his scalp to her belt. Nora is the only seductress in Crane's fiction, indeed the only openly sexual woman, and she is put properly in her place. She tries everything, even open seduction, plying Coleman with strong drink as she entertains him, dressed in a "puzzling gown of . . . Grecian silk," in her subtly lighted room. On the verge of succumbing— "to go to the devil with this girl was not a bad fate" —he is saved by the thought of Marjory, whose name Nora had had the effrontery to mention: his face "instantly stiffened and he looked like a man suddenly recalled to the ways of light."

The book's main interest is in the glimpses it gives of Crane's conception of the journalist's role. Many, however, have found extra interest in comparing Nora Black to Cora Stewart Crane, Crane's common-law wife. He had first met her in 1896 in Jacksonville, Florida, where he had gone preparatory to covering the insurrection in Cuba. Twice married and once divorced, Cora Stewart was the owner of the Hotel de Dream, a successful brothel. "The lady was handsome, of some real refinement, aloof to most," until she met Stephen Crane, with whom she fell deeply in love. He reciprocated. Older than he by some five or six years, eager—as her letters suggest—to care for him and yet tantalizingly unconventional, Cora Stewart had obvious attractions for the young writer who had put such energies into rebellion.

As her biographer suggests, Cora Stewart shared Crane's delight in defying the rules. "One of the greatest pleasures of having been what is called bad is that one has so much to say to the good. Good people love hearing about sin," she wrote. She had flaunted convention by walking out on her well-to-do English husband, Donald Stewart, when he refused her a divorce, and even more by making her way to Jacksonville and establishing her business there. She also shared Crane's romanticism, both its decadent side:

> Sometimes I like to sit at home and read good books, at others
> I must drink absinthe and hang the night hours with scarlet em-
> broideries. I must have music and the sins that march to music

and its idealism:

> Love illuminated by truth, truth warmed through and through by
> love—these perform for us the most blessed thing that one human
> being can do for another.

Cora Stewart also wryly recognized certain "limits of decorum," both in romantic relationships and in business. "Zeus has unquestioned right to Io," she
noted, "but woe betide Io when she suns her heart in the smiles that belong
to Hera." She married her lovers, she was always seen in public with a woman
companion, Mrs. Ruedy, and she promoted the Hotel de Dream as a place
primarily for good food and good conversation. No hard liquor was served,
and Cora Stewart maintained her dignity and her privacy, while charming
men with her wit and conversation.

In Stephen Crane she believed she had found the love she had sought.
He would be her "guiding star. . . . I never realized true happiness or joy
until I met you." Acting on this belief, she gave up what was an established
social position of sorts in Jacksonville, followed Crane to the Greco-Turkish
war (from which she also sent dispatches to the New York *Journal*, writing
as Imogene Carter), and then went to live with him in England as his wife.
The courtship and the marriage were marked by separations and struggles
and, ironically, by a persistent anxiety about the face of propriety to be shown
to the outside world. Pretenses of legal marriage were retailed to friends and
relatives; the bohemians, and apparently Stephen Crane in particular, could
not confront Victorian society head on. Life in England was often difficult.
Both were extravagant, and both loved to entertain. But the guests came in
increasingly unmanageable numbers, and while Stephen Crane played host
and, later, "Baron Brede" (they lived from February 1899 in Brede Place in
Sussex), Cora worried about the bills, about his health, and about ways to
insulate him from his friends so he could work. She also carried on their social
and his business correspondence, and helped the orphaned children of the
improvident Harold Frederic.

Hardest for Cora Crane must have been the realization that Stephen Crane
was not content with their life. Early on, he had described to her his belief
in the evanescence of love:

> Love comes like the tall swift shadow of a ship at night. There

is for a moment, the music of the water's turmoil, a bell, perhaps,
a man's shout, a row of gleaming yellow lights. Then the slow sinking of this mystic shape. Then silence and a bitter silence—the
silence of the sea at night.

When war broke out in Cuba, Crane left England as fast as he could; he did
not return for nine months, and his silence was indeed bitter to Cora. She
had to abandon the dignity she so prized to write frantic letters to the United
States seeking his whereabouts and to publishers seeking money to pay their
bills. He returned to England and to her very slowly. Eighteen months later
he was dead. Cora Crane returned to Jacksonville but her moment was past;
she was never able to reestablish herself successfully in business, made a
disastrous marriage, and died in her mid-forties in 1910.

The "Intrigue" verses, with their apparent allusions to Cora Crane and
her past, were written in Cuba during Crane's long silence. He may also have
returned to the writing of *Active Service* there, completing it when he came
back to England. In its new conception as a romantic story, it too takes swipes
at Cora. Nora Black is not simply a portrait of Cora; the character probably
owes something to the actress Amy Leslie whom Crane had befriended and
who had turned against him, as J. C. Levenson has pointed out. But there
is the echo of the name, the presence of the aged companion, like Cora's Mrs.
Ruedy who had moved to England with her, and the biographical parallel
of Nora Black's work as a "correspondent" during the Greco-Turkish war. The
mixture of styles, sophisticated and crudely vulgar, was also characteristic
of Cora Crane, as Levenson notes.

Nora is by far the liveliest woman in the novel and one of the liveliest
women in any of Crane's fiction. But she is also soundly defeated for her sins.
She arrives on the scene in Greece on her "fat and glossy horse," echoing the
black riders, the "ride of sin," of Crane's early poem. Twice within minutes
of her appearance, Coleman tells her pointedly that she is playing the devil.
Like the woman addressed in "Intrigue," she comes trailing a string of past
conquests. The poet's antagonist/lover is, in one of the worst metaphors in
American poetry, "the beard on another man's face." Nora fares better, but
her aggressive behavior and her fickleness put her beyond the pale. Crane
may not have been able to rescue his past loves from the lives they had chosen
instead of him, but Rufus Coleman will rescue and marry Marjory, and Nora
Black will have to go off in search of her little Greek prince. Art is better
than life.

Nora and the faithless lover of "Intrigue" share with the other women
in Crane's poetry and fiction an inability to be honest—with themselves or,

most important, with others. For Crane, honesty and its attendant virtue loyalty were the only means to redemption. In a much-quoted letter to John Hilliard, probably written in 1896, Crane spelled out his creed:

> I understand that a man is born into the world with his own pair of eyes, and he is not at all responsible for his vision—he is merely responsible for his quality of personal honesty. To keep close to this personal honesty is my supreme ambition. . . . This aim in life struck me as being the only thing worth while. A man is sure to fail at it, but there is something in the failure.

Crane's formulation here parallels a distinction made earlier by his father, the Reverend Jonathan Townley Crane, regarding the relation between the neutral passions of human beings and their responsibility for self-control. In *Holiness, the Birthright of All God's Children* (1874), the elder Crane noted that "to be human is to be endowed with appetites and passions, innocent in themselves but unreasoning, required to be guided by the intellect and the conscience and controlled by the will." His example was Eve, who was to be condemned, not for her desire for the forbidden tree, but for her decision to yield. The premium put by both father and son on the exercise of choice and strength of will is reflected in Crane's assessment of his characters. Circumstances are no excuse, Crane often reiterated—the poor and the dependent have just as much chance to be virtuous. The daughters of Eve clearly have a harder time of it. Self-control, fidelity to a vision of personal honesty and responsibility are not among their gifts.

Contrast, for example, groups of women and men. When men gather in Crane, they are seen to understand each other and to possess a comprehension of the large issues that precludes any unnecessary conversation. When women gather, it is to cackle and rant, to exult in disaster. When Maggie has been found drowned in the East River for her sins, her mother and her acquaintances convene:

> "Yer poor misguided chil' is gone now, Mary, an' let us hope it's fer deh bes'. Yeh'll fergive her now, Mary, won't yehs, dear, all her disobed'ence? All her tankless behavior to her mudder an' all her badness? She's gone where her ter'ble sins will be judged."
> . . . Two or three of the spectators were sniffling, and one was loudly weeping. . . . "She's gone where her sins will be judged," cried the other women, like a choir at a funeral.
> "Deh Lord gives and deh Lord takes away," responded the others.
> "Yeh'll fergive her, Mary!" pleaded the woman in black. The

mourner . . . shook her great shoulders frantically, in an agony
of grief. . . . Finally her voice came and arose like a scream of
pain.   "Oh, yes, I'll fergive her! I'll fergive her!"

When Dr. Trescott, the hero of "The Monster," determines on the path
of righteousness toward the faceless Henry Johnson, he provides the women
of Whilomville with a chance to make noise:

> "Have you heard the news?" cried Carrie Dungen, . . . Her eyes
> were shining with delight.
> "No," answered Martha's sister Kate, . . . "What was it? What
> was it?"
> Carrie appeared triumphantly in the open door. "Oh, there's
> been an awful scene between Doctor Trescott and Jake Winter.
> I never thought Jake Winter had any pluck at all but this morning
> he told the doctor just what he thought of him." . . . "Oh, he called
> him everything. Mrs. Howarth heard it through her front blinds.
> It was terrible, she says. It's all over town now. Everybody knows it."
> "Didn't the doctor answer back?"
> "No! Mrs. Howarth—she says he never said a word . . . But
> Jake gave him jinks, by all accounts."
> "But what did he say?" cried Kate, shrill and excited. She was
> evidently at some kind of feast.

Compare the sound of these scenes among women with Crane's account
of men facing situations of moral and physical danger. Loyalty and
brotherhood characterize the quiet communion of the men in "The Open
Boat":

> The hurt captain, lying against the water-jar in the bow, spoke
> always in a low voice and calmly; but he could never command
> a more ready and swiftly obedient crew than the motley three of
> the dinghy. It was more than a mere recognition of what was best
> for the common safety. There was surely in it a quality that was
> personal and heartfelt. And after this devotion to the commander
> of the boat, there was this comradeship, that the correspondent,
> for instance, who had been taught to be cynical of men, knew even
> at the time was the best experience of his life. But no one said
> that it was so. No one mentioned it.

The silence there is profound, even sacred; the men understand without
speaking, as they do in the stress of battle in *The Red Badge of Courage* and

others of the war stories. There are shrieks and cries there, but they are mechanical—the sounds of war machines—or the cry of pain and the shout of victory. While Maggie's death is celebrated by cannibalistic din, the death of Jim Conklin, through which Henry Fleming learns both the enormity of his sin and his path to redemption, is framed in silence:

> His spare figure was erect; his bloody hands were quietly at his side. He was waiting with patience for something that he had come to meet. He was at the rendezvous. They paused and stood, expectant.
> There was silence.

Crane's two early fictions about women, *Maggie* and *George's Mother,* are loud with the sound of women, betraying their children and bemoaning their betrayal by them. *Maggie* was written when Crane was twenty-one; he published it himself a year later in 1893. He sent copies off to Hamlin Garland and to William Dean Howells, conscious that his small book was in the vein of realism that the older writers prized and hoping that his gesture of literary rebellion—as he saw it—would win him approval. The dedicatory note to Garland was repeated in other copies with only slight modification. Anticipating the reader's shock, he insisted that the book set out to show

> that environment is a tremendous thing . . . and frequently shapes lives regardless. If one proves that theory, one makes room in Heaven for all sorts of souls (notably an occasional street girl) who are not confidently expected to be there by many excellent people.

This attempt to "épater les bourgeois," it scarcely needs saying, is a very limited one. *Maggie* is essentially a tract, written by the son of a gentle Methodist. Crane's father had left the Presbyterian church because he could not accept the doctrine of infant damnation. But he was nonetheless a stringent moralist. Writing in the wake of John Brown's raid on Harper's Ferry, Jonathan Crane had reminded slaves that, whatever their condition, they could feel wronged but must not do wrong, that is, they must not engage in violent revolt.

His son condemned Maggie to death with the same regretful stringency. As Leslie Fiedler pointed out many years ago, Crane took few chances with respectability in his book. By making Maggie so clearly working class, he ensured that her fall into prostitution and her suicide would not unduly disturb the reader. Indeed, the pattern of Maggie's fall might have come directly from the pages of the genteel reformers of the purity crusade. They saw that low wages and the resulting poor living conditions tempted young women to seek for something more. They warned, too, as had Crane's father, against the dangers of alcohol and of popular entertainment, especially the melodramas of the kind to which Pete took Maggie. The first National Purity Congress, held in Baltimore in October 1895, heard many addresses on the relation between alcohol and prostitution and was warned by Josiah Leeds that "impure stage spectacles" bore a direct relation to the spread of the Social Evil. B. O. Flower, editor of the *Arena*, reminded the gathering that the extremes of wealth and poverty to be found in cities could lead only to evil:

> Extreme wealth produces too frequently indolence, high living, the indulgence in wines and liquors, all of which tend to deaden the conscience and stimulate the sensual in man's nature, while the poor, huddled together in overcrowded tenements, lose to a great extent that refinement and modesty so necessary to the development of virtue, and the multitudes of poor girls who are forced to make a living and who are underpaid, too frequently find themselves at the mercy of their employers or are driven through insufficient wages to add to their earnings by yielding to the demands of the men who possess means or influence.

Although Crane expressed only fierce contempt for the do-gooders and reformers, especially against Frances Willard and her temperance crusade, his understanding of what led a girl into the life was exactly what one might expect from a well-brought-up young man. His behavior was rebellious: he associated with prostitutes and women of the demimonde as a way of proving his bohemianism, even though it brought personal risk. But when challenged, he responded out of his background. He defended the honor of Dora Clark, accused of soliciting, and appeared in police court on her behalf. The result was fierce attacks on him by the New York press and personal ostracism. He explained his claim to be married to a woman charged with soliciting: "If it were necessary to avow a marriage to save a girl who is not a prostitute from being arrested as a prostitute, it must be done though the man suffer eternal ruin."

Crane understood the language and the rules in a way that slum inhabitants could not; his rescue attempts could be successful, but Jimmie, Maggie's brother, could not perform the same service for her. He had "an idea that it wasn't common courtesy for a friend to come to one's house and ruin one's sister. But he was not sure how much Pete knew about the rules of politeness." Jimmie's sense of right and wrong is more than his mother or her friends possess, but the comment is nonetheless an easy joke at Jimmie's, and ultimately at Maggie's, expense.

In ascribing Maggie's downfall to what were a conventional set of causes—poverty, the harsh life of the shopgirl, the search for some excitement in a tedious and difficult life—Crane followed a pattern. He breaks it, however, by placing much of the blame for Maggie's fate on the women of the slums. Maggie herself becomes quickly and improbably accomplished in the ways of the streets, knowing to which men to appeal and which to avoid:

> A girl of the painted cohorts of the city went along the street. She threw changing glances at men who passed her, giving smiling invitations to men of rural or untaught pattern and usually seeming sedately unconscious of the men with a metropolitan seal upon their faces.

But Crane makes clear that she is neither successful nor willing at the game; her life as a prostitute is chiefly an occasion for hypocritical self-righteousness on the part of the other female inhabitants of the slums.

As an assault on Christian hypocrisy, Crane liked to recall the attacks on his mother by others when she took in a mother and her child born out of wedlock. Women are incapable, Crane clearly believed, of true charity ("Charity is a toy of women," one poem begins) and even of the kindness and loyalty that should go without saying for an innocent child, and particularly of a mother for her child. Mary Johnson, Maggie's mother, is a drunk, a grotesque, a figure of the angry and malevolent goddess of evil. Her tangled hair calls up the image of the snake, but her threat is not sexual. Her sexuality is only material for a police station joke: " 'Mary, the records of this and other courts show that you are the mother of forty-two daughters who have been ruined. The case is unparalleled in the annals of this court.' " Mary Johnson devours her daughter in her dogged pursuit of her own survival, gorging on self-righteousness and feasting on the clichés of bourgeois morality to justify herself. Her neighbors eagerly join her ravening outbursts, outdoing one another in imaginary tales of Maggie's promiscuity and keening complacently over her death.

George's mother, in the story of that name, would seem to be the opposite of Mary Johnson in every way. Neat, clean, and sanctified, a fierce temperance advocate, she works to retain respectability in the face of looming threats of the slums. Also unlike Mary Johnson, she rejects the other women who come rapaciously ready to join in denunciation of her "wild son. They came to condole her. They sat in the kitchen for hours. She told them of his wit, his cleverness, his kind heart."

But her sanctity and her conception of motherhood are almost as noisy and destructive as Mary Johnson's. She swings from grotesque flirtatiousness to hellfire threats toward George. Obsessed with her own need for him and for his conformity to her idea of what a son should be, she forces him to a prayer meeting and, when that fails, resorts to the final weapon—she dies. Guilty George suffers the drunk's punishment: staring at the wallpaper above his mother's death bed, he sees the brown roses "like hideous crabs crawling upon his brain." His mother has succeeded, not in reforming him, but in giving him a permanent case of guilt.

As has often been noted, one source of this story is an incident between Crane and his mother, Helen Peck Crane. A more fierce Methodist than her husband, she once inveigled her son into attending a prayer meeting; he agreed because he was drunk. The mingled message that the figure of George's mother offers—she invites all the clichés about being brave and pathetic and full of faith, while also uncomprehending of her son—comes perhaps from the story's source. It is not just that Crane uses his mother as a source, but that his perspective here and in *Maggie* remains that of youth, of the son. These women demand to be paid attention to, and their children must heed or suffer.

The sexless, noisy, gossiping women return in "The Monster." Written in 1897 but not published until 1899, this story is a powerful blending of the sun-dappled fiction of the small town with an exploration of its potential for evil. Whilomville—a permutation of Port Jervis, New York, where Crane spent some happy years—was the setting for many of his most whimsical stories: "The Angel Child," "His New Mittens," and others appearing later under the title of *Whilomville Stories* (1900). Most have an edge to them, an awareness of the social hypocrisy in the town, but only in "The Monster" did he use the town as a setting for a morality play. The story turns on a complex moral problem, the question of Dr. Trescott's responsibility to his black serving man, Henry Johnson, who had saved the life of Trescott's son, Jimmie, in a fire. Henry became not only mad but a faceless monster. The question, as Trescott sees it, is one not of charity but of justice.

Henry Johnson is a grotesque of an archetypal kind, a figure at once human and nonhuman. Before the fire, the town could classify Henry with the other blacks in the town and thus dismiss him. Now, faceless, he is suddenly the unknowable in their midst, and they react with anger and resentment. Henry cannot respond, so they direct their fury at Trescott, who refuses to allow Henry to disappear from their lives.

The social life of Whilomville is run by strict if unspoken rules, with clear divisions between the men and the women. The men meet in Reifsnyder's barbershop where they discuss the issues involved in Trescott's determination to help Henry Johnson at whatever risk to himself. Although frightened, the men are at least aware of the importance and value of Trescott's decision; they can understand the abstract considerations that motivate him, although incapable of such courage themselves. The women, however, cannot even begin to understand. They gather in the backyards and kitchens only to gossip, telling tales of those frightened by Henry and whipping themselves into a frenzy of excitement over the affair.

> The overplus of information was choking Carrie. . . . "And, oh, little Sadie Winter is awful sick, . . . And poor old Mrs. Farragut sprained her ankle in trying to climb a fence. And there's a crowd around the jail all the time . . . "
>
> Kate heard the excited newcomer, and drifted down from the novel in her room. . . . "Serves him right if he was to lose all his patients," she said suddenly, in blood-thirsty tones. She snipped her words out as if her lips were scissors.

The men of Whilomville are doubly impotent, before their own inarticulateness and moral inadequacy in the face of Trescott's virtue, and before the simplistic fury of the women. Like the squat and dumb men on the desert, they are made fools of by the women. They take refuge in blaming them. Asking Trescott to send Henry away, the men chorus to each point in their argument, "It's the women."

Like Mary Johnson and the raucous women of the slums, if less coarse, the women of Whilomville are morally and socially deformed. Cannibalistic in their devouring of reputations, they are capable of common action only to destroy. As in *Maggie,* their chief victim is another woman, Grace Trescott, the doctor's wife, who sits alone, bereft and foolish amid her unused teacups as the story ends.

Chief among the women is the "old maid" figure of Martha Goodwin. In several ways, Martha Goodwin resembles the "feminine mule" of Port Jervis whom Crane described in an 1894 letter. That woman had "no more brains than a pig," but whenever "she grunts something dies howling. It may be a girl's reputation or a political party or the Baptist Church but it stops in its tracks and dies." Crane's longtime animus against this woman seems, both in his letter and in his later fictional reincarnations of her, in excess of the cause. He had taken a fifteen-year-old girl out for a buggy ride on Sunday: "Monday the mule addresses me in front of the barber's and says 'You was drivin' Frances out y'day' and grunted. At once all present knew that Frances and I should be hanged on twin gallows for red sins." The "big joke" in all this, Crane gleefully goes on, is that

> this lady in her righteousness is just the grave of a stale lust and every boy in town knows it. She occurred ruin at the hands of a

farmer when we were all 10 or 11. But she is a nice woman and
all her views of all things belong on the table of Moses.

Crane's own self-righteousness, and his pleasure in rehearsing the adolescent snicker over the woman's fate, suggest this attack as a mirror image of the attitude toward women's sexuality seen in the poems. He used this episode with little modification in his early romantic novel, *The Third Violet*, and his obsession with women's past loves has been noted in "Intrigue" and *Active Service*. In "The Monster," he draws again on the episode and the image to create the contradictory figure of Martha Goodwin. Like the feminine mule, Martha has opinions on every large issue and "argued constantly for a creed of illimitable ferocity." She emphasized her opinions with a sniff, which her antagonists received "like a bang over the head, and none was known to recover." She is also and "simply the mausoleum of a dead passion." Her fiancée had died young of smallpox, "which he had not caught from her," and she lives on in the house of her sister and brother-in-law. She is their victim: while her sister Kate is upstairs with her novel, Martha does nearly all the housework "in return for the privilege of existence." Desexed, she can stir up the ashes of passion only in the denunciation of others. But while the women tremble before her savage attacks, they are in "secret revolt" against her. Vulnerable in her dependency, sexless, and without a male defender, "she remained a weak, innocent, and pig-headed creature, who alone would defy the universe if she thought the universe merited the proceeding."

The anger the other women do not dare express openly to Martha, fearful of her sniff, they vent on the unfortunate Grace Trescott, who had developed no sharp tongue to defend herself. Instead she attempts to continue the calls and the teas, the genteel rituals of the town, hoping to retain some of the order that has been broken by her husband's determination. Grace Trescott bears the burden of Dr. Trescott's commitment to justice, his recognition, incomprehensible to the women, that loyalty demands sacrifice. It is her lot to join in that sacrifice without understanding it.

Maggie and "The Monster" are the most vivid illustrations of Crane's conviction of women's incapacity for loyalty, indeed, for moral abstractions of any kind. It is in their disloyalty to each other that women are inferior to men and unredeemable. Not for them the "subtle brotherhood" that allows men to save themselves through mutual self-sacrifice, nor the moment of self-discovery that enables them to transcend past mistakes, as Henry Fleming does, and go on toward redemption. When Maggie reaches the point of self-discovery, it is too late to do anything but, conventionally, to throw herself in the East River. The other women do not reach such a moment.

Crane's happiest letters are to his old schoolmates at Claverack. That boarding school experience seems to have established for him an ideal of companionship and loyalty, a team spirit, that no relationship with a woman or among women could ever match. And, it seems, his view of women never matured far beyond that level of experience. For most of his brief career, the solution was to remove himself, as artist and as man, to the battlefield and the decks of ships, to places where women could not follow.

CHESTER L. WOLFORD

The Anger of Henry Fleming:
The Epic of Consciousness
and The Red Badge of Courage

The Red Badge of Courage establishes Stephen Crane as a writer formally and solidly within the great tradition established and fostered by Homer, Virgil, Milton, and others. While including many of the trappings and conventions and much machinery of formal epic, *The Red Badge* also shares with the epic a more essential quality: the tradition of epic competition. Although greatly oversimplified, a broad review of that tradition would read rather like a social history of western society over the last twenty-five hundred years.

Because it began traditionally with Homer and historically sometime before 400 B.C. in the eastern Mediterranean, the tradition of epic competition is as old as any in western literature. One version of an ancient romantic work called "The Contest of Homer and Hesiod," for example, relates how Homer and Hesiod competed to determine who was the best poet. A comparison of the recitations, as well as the judgment of the audience, indicates that Homer was clearly the better of the two. Yet the king of Chalcis in Euboea, where the contest was reportedly held, awarded the prize to Hesiod, saying that "he who called upon men to follow peace and husbandry should have the prize rather than one who dwelt upon war and slaughter."

While demonstrating the antiquity of epic competition, the story makes another point vital to the tradition and to *The Red Badge*: epics and epic poets do not always compete over literary values. Although the reputations of Virgil and Milton as epic poets rest in part upon how well they compare aesthetically with Homer, nonliterary factors such as cultural and religious values also claim the attention of these men. The most important of these

From *The Anger of Stephen Crane: Fiction and the Epic Tradition.* © 1983 by the University of Nebraska Press.

values for the epic is the different ideal of heroism held by each poet, particularly regarding the object of man's duty. The Homeric epics may be termed "individual" because they tend to glorify the individual man. Virgil's is a "group" epic because it glorifies Rome and defines the state as a more worthy object of duty than the individual. Milton attempts, among other things, to glorify a Puritan God and to justify worthiness in his sight as the object of man's duty. To the degree that Milton saw man's task as an attempt to reproduce God's kingdom in the self and community of Christians, *Paradise Lost* and *Paradise Regained* become "group" epics. One way, then, to look at the history of the West is as a movement from man being accountable only for himself—man as individualistic and egocentric—to man as part of something larger, more enduring and significant than himself.

Each of these views finds an embodiment in a great epic poet's notion of heroism, for heroism consists of fulfilling the demands of duty. The Homeric hero ascribes to the code of *areté*, which demands that he strive ceaselessly for the first prize. The driving force behind all the hero's actions, *areté* often connotes values different from Roman and Christian virtues. Virtues lauded over the last fifteen hundred years and more—loyalty, honesty, charity, fair play—are simply not part of the code of *areté*; Achilles deserted the field and his friends and spent much of the war in an adolescent funk, and Odysseus was a liar and a cheat, but both were great warriors and so have the highest *areté*.

What distinguishes Virgil's Aeneas from Homeric heroes is not the greatness of his deeds but the reasons for performing them. Virgil's epithet for Aeneas is "pius," a term denoting more than "pious" as Aeneas is also "dutiful." Careful to pour appropriate libations for the gods, Aeneas also is concerned for his family and his destiny. Seeker of peace, invincible in war, believer in law, Aeneas is the heroic ideal of the *Romanum Imperium* of Augustus.

To explain how Aeneas, a second-level Homeric hero in the *Iliad,* became a metaphor for Rome in the *Aeneid* would require several volumes of social, intellectual, and literary history that would carry one from Attic to Roman civilizations. The problem for Virgil, however, was that Homer still dominated the genre in Augustan Rome and his heroes were still revered. As a result, Virgil was forced to compete unevenly with Homer. If Rome were superior to Homeric Greece, then the great Roman epic would have to be superior to the Homeric epics. Virgil succeeded, at least politically, by elevating the Roman hero and debasing the Homeric, elevating *pietas* and debasing *areté*. Thus Turnus, *alius Achilles,* embodies *areté*, and when Aeneas kills him in the poem's final lines, Virgil metaphorically "kills" Achilles, *areté*, and the

Homeric epic. Later Christian epic poets such as Tasso, Camoëns, Dante, and Ariosto also despise *areté*—which they saw as almost identical to *hubris*—and show their contempt by assigning it as a quality belonging to their heroes' enemies. Milton's Satan belongs to this type, and in spite of his attractiveness as a Homeric or Shelleyan hero, he is nevertheless a personification of evil. Milton's concept of heroism and duty is as complex as his use of the epic medium, but it is also clear that genuine heroism lies in "true patience and heroic martyrdom." The real Christian hero seeks glory by following the New Testament and dedicates his deeds *ad majoram gloriam Dei.* How one plays the game determines whether one wins or loses.

When Crane includes these notions of heroism and duty in *The Red Badge,* he undertakes a task crucial to writing epics. Because these concepts of heroism and duty are among the most influential in Western history, when Crane denigrates and replaces them, he rewrites, in a very real sense, the cultural history of the West.

INWARD REPUDIATIONS

The first chapter of *The Red Badge* presents heroic ideals in the mind of Henry Fleming, a "youth" inclined by instinct toward *areté* but checked by "religious and secular education" so that he feels himself to be a part of something much larger than himself. Henry is introduced into the story and is immediately engaged in a debate over "some new thoughts that had lately come to him." On the one hand, he sees himself in expressly Homeric terms, with "peoples secure in the shadow of his eagle-eyed prowess." In retrospect, he remembers having "burned several times to enlist. Tales of great movements shook the land. They might not be distinctly Homeric, but there seemed to be much glory in them. He had read of marches, sieges, conflicts, and he had longed to see it all. His busy mind had drawn for him large pictures extravagant in color, lurid with breathless deeds." On the other hand, his mother, the voice of Christian-group ideals, "had discouraged him." Her advice upon his enlistment is the advice of the group: "Don't go a-thinkin' you can lick the hull rebel army at the start, because yeh can't. Yer just one little feller amongst a hull lot of others, and yeh've got to keep quiet an' do what they tell yeh." Contrary to Henry's Grecian mood—he would rather have heard "about returning with his shield or on it" —his mother's relationship to Christianity is everywhere apparent. Her only remark upon hearing of Henry's enlistment is "The Lord's will be done," and when he leaves she says simply, "The Lord'll take keer of us all."

As a surrogate mother, the army too puts a damper on his heated individualism. Before leaving home, "he had felt growing within him the strength to do mighty deeds of arms," but after spending "months of monotonous life in a camp," Henry comes "to regard himself as part of a vast blue demonstration."

Throughout the first half of *The Red Badge,* the competition between the individualism of Henry's *areté* and the collectivism of *pietas* and "heroic martyrdom" swings between extremes. In his first engagement, Henry seems finally to give in to the standards of the group: "He suddenly lost concern for himself and forgot to look at a menacing fate. He became not a man but a member. He felt that something of which he was a part—a regiment, an army, a cause, or a country—was in crisis. He was welded into a common personality which was dominated by a single desire." Soon, the group becomes even more important to him than the causes: "He felt the subtle battle brotherhood more potent even than the cause for which they were fighting. It was a mysterious fraternity."

Much has been made of Henry's joining the subtle brotherhood, but few remember that when the enemy makes a second charge against the regiment, the mysterious fraternity dissolves under an individuality revived by Henry's sense of self-preservation. He turns tail and runs. Although Achilles has more grace and style, the effect is the same in either case: both Henry and Achilles desert their friends in the field. To say, as many do, that Henry should be damned for his desertion is to speak from an historically narrow perspective; from an Homeric standpoint, one cannot be so quick to judge. In fact, no moral judgments necessarily result from Henry's flight. If Henry can get away with it (he does), if no one finds out about it (no one does), and if later he can perform "great deeds" (he does), then that is all that matters. By the end of the sixth chapter, Henry's individualism, his Homeric sense, seems to have won a limited victory—victory because Henry has escaped being subsumed by the group, limited because his sense of shame dogs him throughout the novel.

In the novel's first half the battle for Henry's allegiance to Homeric or Christian-group values occurs in Henry's mind. In the first six chapters, Henry's conflicting feelings need little prodding; in the second six, the action of the novel intensifies, as do attacks on his individualism. In this quarter of the novel, Henry enters the "forest chapel," sees Jim Conklin die in a Christ-like way, and is mentally and verbally assaulted by the "tattered man." Here, too, he receives his "red badge of courage."

It should not be surprising in light of the epic structure that this section of *The Red Badge* is filled with religious imagery. Much critical ink has been spilt in a controversy over whether or not Crane, given his naturalistic bent and nihilist vision, intends Jim Conklin, for example, to represent Christ, or the tattered man to represent the Christian-group ideal; many feel that Crane himself was confused about it and that the novel fails because he fails to resolve the problem. These chapters mark what ultimately becomes a failure of the Christian-group value system—with two thousand years of indoctrination behind it—to make Henry Fleming return to the fold. It is not Crane's intent to have the reader see things in a religious way, but to see Henry succumb to the pathetic fallacy of Christian-colored glasses.

Arriving at a spot deep in the woods, Henry hears the trees "sing a hymn of twilight. . . . There was a lull in the noises of insects as if they had bowed their beaks and were making a devotional pause. There was silence save for the choruses of trees." Henry now sees things through a "religious half light," and the forest seems to form a "chapel" complete with "arching boughs," "green doors," and a "brown carpet."

When Crane places more emphasis on character and action than upon natural scenes, Christian morality and group ethics are even more strongly merged. Both value systems require humility, love, awe, and admiration for something perceived as greater than and outside of the individual. In chapters 6 to 12, the screw is tightened on Henry's conscience, demanding both complete subjection and unqualified support. The first person Henry sees after leaving the forest is the tattered man, who, for Henry, embodies the Christian-group ideal. The tattered man is introduced by a dignified and classical anaphora as if he were the subject of an ancient fable: "There was a tattered man. . . ." This archetypal follower listens to an officer's "lurid tale" with "much humility." Rough as the ragged private looks, his voice is as "gentle as a girl's," and when he speaks it is "timidly." His "pleading" eyes are described in a simile bearing a Christian symbol that could not have escaped Crane; they are "lamblike." With a general "air of apology in his manner," the tattered man is so humble, timid, and conventionally feminine that he becomes a caricature of a Christian-group member. Even his physiognomy betrays an overwhelming love for the group. "His homely face was suffused with a light of love for the army which was to him all things powerful and beautiful." Crane here takes standard emotional slither from the rhetoric of nineteenth-century religious writers' descriptions of people saved at camp meetings and attaches it to the army. All of the tattered man's questions are uttered "in a brotherly tone," and his "lean features wore an expression of awe and admiration." In short, he must have been meant to be a caricature, for even his breathing has in it a "humble admiration."

It is also clear that Henry sees Jim Conklin in a "religious half light." Stallman's original reading of Conklin as Christ is fundamentally correct if one understands that it is Henry and not Crane who sees Conklin as Christ.

Few figures in American literature have a better claim to the trappings of Christ's Passion than does Jim Conklin. His initials are J. C., he is wounded in the side, he dies on a hill, he is a "devotee of a mad religion," and his death stirs "thoughts of a solemn ceremony." Those who deny that Conklin is a Christ-figure usually do so by pointing out that Conklin is a loud, cracker-crunching, rumormonger. Such evidence is specious, since these qualities are part of Jim only before he became "not a man but a member" by staying on the line during the battle. Some also forget that Crane's intent is to show that Henry sees Conklin in this way, not that Conklin is that way.

One way to place the various episodes of the first half into a perspective of the moral and social competition between Christian-group values and the Homeric ideal of individualism (*areté*) may be to describe that epic competition as a representation of the psychology of Christian conversion from an egocentric individualism to an altruistic membership in the flock. The pattern is similar; as a moral being, man in Christian process moves from the commission of sin to guilt, to alienation, to a desire for expiation, to confession, and finally to redemption. In the end, the process fails to redeem Henry for Christianity, but it does give him a rough time of it, and it organizes the epic competition and psychology of the novel's first half.

Three particular episodes are representative of this psychological movement. The episodes with Mrs. Fleming, Jim Conklin, and the tattered man each appear to bring Henry steadily closer to rejecting his Homeric individuality while ultimately functioning ironically to force his acceptance of *areté*. By the time he is hit on the head and receives his "red badge of courage," Henry has sloughed off the Christian-group concept of heroism. His red badge is, however, not ironical in that he receives it for an act of cowardice; rather it is an outward sign—what the Greeks called *geras*—of his accomplishment in rejecting two thousand years of social and religious indoctrination. An epic feat.

Occurring in the first chapter, the "Mrs. Fleming" episode serves to increase Henry's feelings of sin and guilt over his Homeric sense of selfish individuality which encompasses egoism, insensitivity, and the pursuit of personal glory at all costs—*areté*. The episode opens with Henry in his hut (and *in medias res*) remembering his earlier thoughts about "breathless deeds," his "burning to enlist," and his having "despaired of witnessing a Greeklike struggle."

Mrs. Fleming is a stereotype of the pious, hard-working, long-suffering, farm boy's mother. Her views are Christian-group oriented and come from "deep conviction." Her "ethical motives" are "impregnable." Guilt and remorse over his insensitivity toward his mother work on Henry as he remembers a scene from his leave-taking: "When he had looked back from the gate, he had seen his mother kneeling among the potato parings. Her brown face, up-raised, was stained with tears, and her spare form was quivering." The effect on Henry is predictable: "He bowed his head and went on, feeling suddenly ashamed of his purposes." Significantly, he is not so much ashamed of enlisting as he is of his purposes, his longing for the glory road of individual heroism that scatters the hurt feelings and genuine needs of others along the road-side. Christians would accuse Henry of *hubris*; Augustan Romans would not chide him for enlisting but for having done so without thought to duty and family; Homeric Greeks would have wondered what all the fuss was about, shrugged their shoulders, and remarked that while the action might be a lit-tle sad, it was also probably necessary: how else become a hero? Unlike Homeric heroes, however, Henry leaves for war carrying in his soul the cultural burdens of twenty centuries of self-condemnation succumbing to *areté*.

It is important to emphasize the universal qualities of the novel in general and of Henry Fleming in particular. He is at once common and uncommon; he is Man rebelling against his Mother, Mankind (or at least the archetypal American in the archetypal American novel) attempting to slough off the Past. In the American experience this last action ties Henry closely to the transcendental movement, as well as to such archetypal figures as Huck Finn, Natty Bumppo, Rip Van Winkle, and a host of other American heroes. The difference is that unlike Twain, Cooper, and Irving, Crane is using the formal epic ironically to destroy the traditions of heroism, and epic competition is used because its very purpose is to disparage what the past has considered to be the highest expression of man's duty, courage.

The Jim Conklin episode carries Henry a step further in the process by adding to sin and guilt the anguish of alienation and the desire for expiation through good works. After deserting the regiment and wandering through the forest, Henry joins a band of wounded men moving toward the rear. These men have stood their ground—for God and country possibly, for the group certainly. Their wounds seem to symbolize their sacrifices and their devotion to duty. Seeing them this way, Henry feels alienated: "At times he regarded the wounded soldiers in an envious way. . . . He wished that he, too, had a wound, a red badge of courage." Such a badge would grant to Henry membership and acceptance in the group, would assuage his guilt and close the gap between himself and the others caused by his alienation. Henry's anguish is greater now than during the earlier episode: "He felt his shame could be viewed. He was continually casting sidelong glances to see if the men were contemplating the letters of guilt he felt burned in his brow." At this stage Henry is Stephen Crane's Dimmesdale, and the only difference between the two is that Crane's character ultimately is able to "put the sin at a distance." Hawthorne's protagonist never can.

Feeling that he bears the Mark of the Beast, Henry is then confronted by Jim Conklin's wounds, and in his already anguished state, Henry is quite ready to see in Jim an exceptional Christian devotion to duty and sacrifice for the group. Jim's actions, however, deny Henry expiation and even serve further to heighten his anxiety. Henry's attempts to receive absolution are repulsed, for Jim only wants to be left alone to die: "The youth put forth anxious arms to assist him, but the tall soldier went firmly on as if propelled. . . . The youth had reached an anguish where the sobs scorched him. He strove to express his loyalty. . . . The youth wished his friend to lean upon him, but the other always shook his head and strangely protested. 'No—no—no—leave me be—leave me be— '. . . . and all the youth's offers he brushed aside." Henry's view of Jim as a Christ is Henry's alone. The youth's attempts to assuage his guilt in a bath of atonement fail; although he asks, he does not receive—Jim Conklin will have none of it. All that remains is Henry's very real and painful desire for redemption. Redemption itself is as far away as ever.

Henry's Christian-group consciousness is pushed to its limits in the "tattered man" episode. There are two "sins" here: one is Henry's refusal to confess his earlier desertion of the regiment, and the other is his desertion of the tattered man, an act which redoubles his guilt. When Henry meets the tattered man, the latter repeatedly asks him, "Where yeh hit?" This question, asked over and over again, causes Henry to feel the "letters of guilt" burned, Dimmesdale-like, into his forehead. Instead of causing Henry to repent, however, the letters merely force him to desert the wounded tattered man and leave him to wander off into the fields to die. Immediately after deserting the tattered man, Henry's guilt reaches almost unbearable proportions: "The simple questions of the tattered man had been knife thrusts to him. They asserted a society that probes pitilessly at secrets until all is apparent. . . . He could not keep his crime concealed in his bosom. . . . He admitted that he could not defend himself." Believing that "he envied those men whose bodies lay strewn" on the field, he explicitly wants to be redeemed: "A moral vindication was regarded by the youth as a very important thing."

Confused, guilt-ridden, and afraid that the group may discover his "sin," Henry's mind goes through, as in the first chapter, the same metronomic movement between the demands of the group and the desires of the individual, but with more pain. Henry's anguish remains severe throughout the eleventh chapter. In the twelfth chapter, however, this changes.

Chapter 12 is the last chapter of the first half of *The Red Badge*. Like the end of the first half of the *Iliad,* the *Odyssey,* the *Aeneid, Paradise Lost,* and other epics, it includes both a culmination of the first half and a preparation for the second. In the twelfth book of the *Iliad,* the Trojans have broken into the Greek encampment. They are never again so close to victory. In the *Odyssey,* the hero nears the end of his wanderings and sets off in the next book for a final successful junket to Ithaca, where he will lay plans to set his house in order. In the *Aeneid,* Aeneas is about to land in Italy, thus putting himself in a position to fulfill his destiny by founding the Roman nation. In *Paradise Lost,* the battle in heaven ends; Satan and his angels have fallen into Hell, and the stage is set for the second half: the fall of man. Similarly, in *The Red Badge,* Henry completes his epic of return by sloughing off his Christian-group conscience: he accepts his individuality, and he is then prepared to battle the group in the second half.

Henry is "reborn" after being hit on the head in chapter 12. The language of the episode is carefully, even poetically, rendered to represent rebirth. After watching a group of retreating soldiers, Henry runs down from a rise, grabs one of the soldiers, and is clouted for his trouble:

> [The other soldier] adroitly and fiercely swung his rifle. It crushed upon the youth's head. The man ran on.
>
> The youth's fingers had turned to paste upon the other's arm. The energy was smitten from his muscles. He saw the flaming wings of lightning flash before his vision. There was a deafening rumble of thunder within his head.
>
> Suddenly his legs seemed to die. He sank writhing to the ground. He tried to arise. In his efforts against the numbing pain he was like a man wrestling with a creature of the air.
>
> There was a sinister struggle.
>
> Sometimes he would achieve a position half erect, battle with the air for a moment, and then fall again, grabbing at the grass. His face was of a clammy pallor. Deep groans were wrenched from him.
>
> At last, with a twisting movement, he got upon his hands and knees, and from thence, like a babe trying to walk, to his feet. . . . he went lurching over the grass.
>
> He fought an intense battle with his body. His dulled senses wished him to swoon and he opposed them stubbornly, his mind portraying unknown dangers and mutilations if he should fall upon the field. He went tall soldier fashion.

Structurally, the passage focuses first on the falling away of the old in a meta phorical death. Henry loses his sight, his hearing, and then his ability to stand erect. In the middle is a five-word, one-sentence paragraph describing a "sinister struggle" between life and death. From there, the reborn Henry gets up on his hands and knees "like a babe," and finally is able to walk. In spite of the almost allegorical nature of the passage, its essence remains one of a very physical, almost literal, and, most important, quite individual rebirth.

One cannot help but think that the anthropological cast of the passage is intentional. At least, it demonstrates that Crane, however unconsciously, was aware of the consequences for thought of the Darwinian revolution. For Henry, as for mankind, the traditional past could no longer provide solace. Indeed, as the second half of *The Red Badge* shows, the traditional past had to be rolled up and replaced by naturalism and impressionism. These terms, given Holton's appraisal of elements shared by definitions of the former and Nagel's definition of impressionism, can be seen in some lights as nearly synonymous and as twin effects of *Origin of the Species* and of the dissemination of other scientific discoveries.

The action reported in this passage is unlike anything else in the book. Except for a later instance when he pushes another fellow, it is Henry's only hostile physical encounter in the novel. Certainly this is not Christian-group combat; it is especially unusual for those engaged in modern warfare. Prior to this point all battles have been described as remote from the individual. Cannons roar at each other, and men shoot at "vague forms" shifting and running through the smoke of many rifles. Always the action has been described in terms of one group charging toward or retreating from another. Moreover, his adversary fights under the same flag as Henry.

Here, for the first time, is a representation of a "Greeklike struggle" that once had been merely a part of Henry's dreams. It has not developed as Henry had expected, and may not be distinctly Homeric, but it is close to primitive hand-to-hand combat, and bears little resemblance to the "mighty blue machine" of the group. For the first time, Henry struggles with another man. Further, Henry's wound is unusual for participants in a modern, group war. Henry's wound is not from a bullet, but from the butt end of a modern weapon used as the most ancient of weapons; as one fellow observes, "It's raised a queer lump as if some feller lammed yeh on the head with a club."

Henry's wandering off "tall soldier fashion" after receiving the blow on the head does not mean that Henry has been converted to a group view of things. To see Jim as a Christian-group figure is to make the same mistake Henry made. Strip away the dramatic symbolism of Henry's former vision of Conklin and one is left with a man dying, alone, unwilling to be helped, and as afraid of mutilation as any Homeric hero. Speech and action are "real"; Henry's interpretation of them may not be. When Henry thus goes "tall soldier fashion" it is not necessarily as a Christ-figure. Henry is in no shape at this point to interpret events; in this instance, the information comes directly from the narrator. The dying Jim Conklin and the wounded Henry Fleming are linked, or seem to be linked, only by a desire to escape the group.

Wandering in the gathering darkness, Henry is finally given direction by an epic guide. Like the role of the captain in "The Reluctant Voyagers," the function of the "cheery man" is traditional to the machinery of epic. As Ariadne helps Theseus, Thetis comforts Achilles, Athena aids Odysseus, Venus supports and guides Aeneas, and Virgil leads Dante, so the cheery man helps Henry to gain self-control, and, as Gibson points out, places him in a position to confront those forces which he otherwise would have little power to oppose but which he must overcome in order to complete his epic task. The cheery man leads Henry back to the regiment.

Unlike the two men in "The Reluctant Voyagers," Henry appreciates, albeit somewhat after the fact, the cheery man's help. And well he should, for as he staggers towards the campfires of his regiment in the beginning of the second half of *The Red Badge,* he has nearly done the impossible. In a sense, he has performed more courageously than Achilles. Peliades had only to reach his goal of *areté*, while Fleming had first to throw off his sense of sin and alienation. On one level, he has suffered all the slings and "arrows of scorn" that can be shot at an individual by the archers of conscience, guilt, and alienation from the group. On another level, Henry has forced his way back through two millennia of nationalism and Christianity. Such an act is impossible for an ordinary man. To oppose and overcome, even to a limited degree, the teachings of secular and religious culture is an almost incredible, even epic, feat.

OUTWARD WARS

Yet the battle is only half won. As the first twelve chapters are concerned with Henry's struggle to gain individuality of mind, the second half of *The Red Badge* concerns Henry's conflict with the same forces in the externalized, "outside" world. In terms of the epic of consciousness, the first half concerns Henry's escape from the cave, his coming to consciousness, and his gaining self-control, that is, coming to terms with alienation from the other—the group and the rest of the material world—and the fact of death. Having come to terms internally in the first half, he is ready to confront the other externally in the second half. Here, as in the *Aeneid*, the hero is confronted with a competition between his new-found values and an externalized embodiment and proponent of the value system he has recently overcome internally. In the second half of the *Aeneid*, Aeneas must confront, battle, and finally defeat the Roman version of the Homeric ideal of *areté* embodied in Turnus. In the last half of *The Red Badge*, Henry must confront, engage, and overcome Wilson, who has not only been "converted" and initiated into the group, but also has become the embodiment of Christian-group consciousness and its value system.

When Henry returns to confront the group, to enter into the midst of the "subtle brotherhood," he manages to resist its attempts to "initiate" him into membership. Henry seems aware at this point of the nature of this confrontation, because "there was a sudden sinking of his forces. He thought he must hasten to produce his tale to protect him from the missiles already at the lips of his redoubtable comrades." The "information" is a baldfaced lie: "Yes, yes. I've—I've had an awful time. I've been all over. Way over on the right. . . . I got separated from the regiment. Over on the right, I got shot. In the head. I never saw such fighting." The lie works, and Henry seems to become the lost sheep returned to the fold.

Wilson, the sentinel who recognizes Henry staggering into camp, seems remarkably changed. Henry now views Wilson much as he had viewed the tattered man, only with colder eyes. In the first chapter, Wilson acted the part of a *miles gloriosus,* a parody of Achilles. In that chapter, which mirrors the first book of the *Iliad,* Wilson engaged Jim Conklin in an argument. Like Achilles and Agamemnon, "they came near to fighting over" their differences. Wilson also spent much time bragging about his prowess in battle. Now, however, Wilson seems to embody Christian-group values. When first seen in chapter 13, he is standing guard over the regiment. Upon recognizing Henry, he lowers his rifle and welcomes the youth back: "There was husky emotion in his voice." Later, while dressing Henry's wound, Wilson acts out the feminine role of the soothing and clucking mother hen who welcomes one of her lost chicks back to the coop: "He had the bustling ways of an amateur nurse. He fussed around." When Wilson puts his cloth on Henry's head, it feels to the youth "like a tender woman's hand."

Because he didn't run, Wilson was subsumed by that "regiment, army, cause," or country; he joined the "subtle brotherhood," the "mysterious fraternity born of the smoke and danger of death." At the beginning of the battle neither Henry nor Wilson had gained a genuine sense of individuality; both at that point were vulnerable to the group. Because he ran, Henry was excluded from the ego-annihilating forces which Wilson joined.

As a result, Henry and Wilson are now two very different kinds of men. Wilson, who had earlier jumped at any chance to get into an argument or a fight, now stops a fight between two men; he explains to Henry, "I hate t' see th' boys fightin' 'mong themselves." Henry, however, feels no such obligation to become a peacemaker; he laughs and reminds Wilson of an earlier fight the formerly loud soldier had had with "that Irish feller." Certain that he would be killed, Wilson had given Henry a packet of letters before the first battle with instructions that they be sent home after his "imminent" death. The contrast between Wilson's new-found humility and Henry's arrogance appears when Wilson asks for the letters back. Wilson flushes and fidgets, "suffering great shame." When Henry gives them back, he tries "to invent a remarkable comment upon the affair. He could conjure up nothing of sufficient point. He was compelled to allow his friend to escape unmolested with his packet. And for this he took unto himself considerable credit. It was a generous thing. . . . The youth felt his heart grow more strong and stout. He had never been compelled to blush in such a manner for his acts; he was an individual of extraordinary virtues." There is a double irony here. On one level, the passage mocks Henry, but on another, Henry is essentially correct. He has not been "compelled" to undergo the humility of confession. He has overcome in large measure the need for communal redemption of guilt and shame. He does, indeed, have extraordinary "virtues," but they are the "virtues" of *areté*, pride, and individualism.

As they begin the second day of battle, Henry and Wilson are very soon recognized by the group as entirely different kinds of heroes. First, Henry is transfigured by *menos*, the animal-like battle-rage of Homeric heroes: "Once, he, in his intent hate, was almost alone and was firing when all those near him ceased. He was so engrossed in his occupation that he was not aware of a lull." One man derides him for not stopping when the others had, but the lieutenant (whose "voice" had been described as expressing a "divinity") praises Henry in animistic terms. "By heavens, if I had ten thousand wildcats like you I could tear th' stomach outa this war in less'n a week!" Finally, Henry receives the recognition from the group that Homeric heroes seek. He is viewed as someone separate, distinct, and most important, superior: "They now looked upon him as a war-devil," they are "awe-struck."

Wilson is a hero of a different age. Henry does not incite the group to action; his only concern is for his own heroism. Wilson, the hero of the group, serves this purpose: "The friend of the youth aroused. Lurching suddenly forward and dropping to his knees, he fired an angry shot at the persistent woods. This action awakened the men. They huddled no more like sheep . . . they began to move forward."

Wilson has become the leader of his flock, and Henry has become a Homeric "war devil."

There are a number of confrontations between Henry and Wilson in their respective roles as individual and group heroes. The morning after Henry's return to camp, for example, Wilson "tinkers" with the bandage on Henry's head, trying to keep it from slipping. Friendly, consoling, and helpful, Wilson is berated by an unfriendly, arrogant Henry: "Gosh-dern it . . . you're the hangdest man I ever saw! You wear muffs on your hands. Why in good thunderation can't you be more easy? . . . Now, go slow, an' don't act as if you was nailing down carpet." Henry seems already to have gained superiority over his counterpart: "He glared with insolent command at his friend."

Later, when Henry remembers the letters Wilson had given him, he again feels his superiority and thinks in terms of dominance: "He had been possessed of much fear of his friend, for he saw how easily questionings could make holes in his feelings. . . . He now rejoiced in the possession of a small weapon with which he could prostrate his comrade at the first signs of cross-examination. He was master." Wilson remains a symbol to Henry of Christian-group conscience throughout the second half, and Henry never completely overcomes his own Christian-group sense. It dogs him.

The crucial confrontation between the two heroes is a face-to-face physical encounter on the battlefield. It occurs, fittingly, in a contest to determine who will carry the flag across the field in the charge. For Wilson, the traditional approach to the flag as a symbol of a group is most appropriate. Possession of the flag would mean that Wilson had reached the goal of all group epic heroes: to become the idealized symbol of the group. For Henry, the flag is also a symbol of the group. But Homeric heroes strive after *geras*, the prize, the symbol by which they are acknowledged by the group as superior. Possession of the flag would mean that he had fulfilled the aspect of *areté* that demands that he achieve supremacy over the group. Consequently, the flag becomes for Henry "a goddess, radiant, that bent its form with an imperious gesture to him. It was a woman . . . that called to him with the voice of his hopes."

Since the flag is a symbol both for the group and for the superior individual, it is natural, when the bearer is shot, that both Henry and Wilson should go after the flag. It is also inevitable, although slightly contrived, that they should reach it at the same time: "He [Henry] made a spring and a clutch at the pole. At the same instant, his friend grabbed it from the other side."

Neither Henry nor Wilson relinquishes the flagpole and a "small scuffle" ensues. For Henry, however, possession of the flag means so much in terms of dominance over his peers that he has no compunctions about using force against his comrade: "The youth roughly pushed his friend a way."

In gaining the flag, Henry has defeated his Christian-group rival and the value system Wilson champions. Henry has gained supremacy over his peers, achieving his *areté*. Yet the victory is not complete: there is still the enemy's flag. Were Henry to claim that flag as well, he would be proven superior not only to his peers, but also to the collective body. Henry fails. Although there is much heroism in becoming individual, one is never completely freed from the group. Its influences, physical and mental, remain forever. Although Henry has equaled or surpassed the deeds of Achilles and Odysseus, although he has overcome in large measure the long stony sleep of Christian-group culture and heritage, he fails to gain a complete victory. It is as if Henry knows what its possession would mean: "The youth had centered the gaze of his soul upon that other flag. Its possession would be high pride." But Wilson, that champion of the group, had dogged Henry across the battlefield and beat Henry to it by springing like Christ the Panther: "The youth's friend . . . sprang at the flag as a panther at prey. He pulled at it, and wrenching it free, swung up its red brilliancy with a mad cry of exultation."

In terms of the epic tradition, Henry's possessing the other flag could have meant possibly a complete victory for the Homeric epic over the social epic after two thousand years. It might also have meant a winning back of the heroic, individual "soul" after two millennia of suppression by Christian-group value systems, both political and spiritual. But, as the later Scratchy Wilson of "The Bride Comes to Yellow Sky" and the Swede of "The Blue Hotel" discover, such a victory is fleeting at best and always illusory. Wilson may have lost an individual encounter with Henry, but he has also proven that the group cannot be completely defeated by the individual.

VICTORIES

The epic tradition demands that a writer replace former concepts of epic heroism with his own if he wishes to be more than a mere imitator. In nearly all of Crane's best work, his idea of heroism is his ideal of personal honesty. Repeatedly, Crane measures his characters against this standard; Henry Fleming measures as well as any.

More than any other sort of writer, one whose work has epic dimensions lends to his fictional heroes his own supreme ambition; so much is this so, in fact, that the poet himself may be considered the ultimate hero of his own epic, and is sometimes difficult to separate from the fictional hero. For millennia the epic poet has been set apart from his fellows by his abilities, but especially by the intensity of his vision and by the degree to which he believes in it. For Crane, keeping close to his vision, in terms both of apprehension and of comprehension, is the standard not only of honesty but of heroism as well.

The desire to see clearly runs through *The Red Badge of Courage*. Henry in particular seeks continually to perceive with his own eyes. There are more than two hundred references in *The Red Badge* to Henry seeing, not seeing, or trying to see. However, his sight tends always to be obscured either by the group, which limits what the individual can see, or by a kind of Homeric hero complex in which Henry feels that an individual can see everything. Each is a form of blindness and each corresponds to one of the two epic value systems. There is an implication throughout most of the novel (the implication becomes explicit in the last chapter) that history is little more than an individual interpretation of events raised to a level of cultural reporting and collective interpreting. Both as individual and as representative man, Henry makes his own specific interpretations of events. On the other hand, those interpretations are also colored by epic concepts. If the individual's interpretation is deluded, so is the epic's, and vice versa.

Since Crane uses "vision" as a metaphor for his own particular notion of heroism, former notions of epic heroism are first debased and then replaced by the use of images and references to seeing. One of the value systems attacked in *The Red Badge* is the Christian-group view, which obscures and distorts the attempts of the individual to "see." The group, in the form of the army or the brigade or the regiment, is constantly associated with smoke or fog. As Henry is about to move into his first engagement, he identifies the fog with the army; indeed, the fog seems to emanate from the group: "The youth thought the damp fog of early morning moved from the rush of a great body of troops." The same image is used in the opening sentence of the novel: "The cold passed reluctantly from the earth, and the retiring fogs revealed an army stretched out on the hills, resting." Smoke is even more often associated with the group. Although realistic in a novel about war before the invention of smokeless powder, the image is used for much more than verisimilitude. At one point the position of an entire brigade is identified only by reference to the position of a blanket of smoke: "A brigade ahead of them went into action with a rending roar. It was as if it had exploded. And, thereafter, it lay stretched in the distance behind a long gray wall that one was obliged to look twice at to make sure that it was smoke." Not only is smoke identified with the brigade, but smoke also seems to give it protection.

The group is also seen in terms of darkness, snakes, and monsters, which in epics and archetypes of the unconscious are usually identified with evil. As the army is forming to march into battle, Henry perceives the group: "From off in the darkness, came the trampling of feet. The youth could occasionally see dark shadows that moved like monsters." As the "monsters" moved off in columns, "there was an occasional flash and glimmer of steel from the backs of all these crawling reptiles." And the "two long, thin, black columns" appear "like two serpents crawling from the cavern of the night." The men of the group themselves sometimes appear "satanic" to Henry.

Most often, however, the smoke of the group obscures and distorts Henry's vision. With the smoke of "the war atmosphere" around him in his first engagement, Henry had "a sensation that his eye-balls were about to crack like hot stones." His desire to see is constantly getting in the way of his assimilation into the group, but he can never get an unobstructed view and his other senses are stifled, almost annihilated by the physical and metaphorical "smoke" of the group. Against this smoke Henry directs more of his anger than against a charging enemy: "Buried in the smoke of many rifles his anger was directed not so much against the men he knew were rushing toward him as against the swirling battle phantoms which were choking him, stuffing their smoke robes down his parched throat."

The group has the ability to hide reality from the individual. The group takes away the individual's unobstructed use of his senses—the only means he has of perceiving the world around him. While surrounded by "smoke," a man cannot "see," and will behave in the way the group wants him to behave. Shortly before Henry becomes "not a man but a member," for example, he and the regiment are moving rapidly forward to a "struggle in the smoke": "In this rush they were apparently all deaf and blind."

After he has run, been hit on the head, and returned to the group, Henry sees the regiment in a more sinister aspect. After spending the night in sleep Henry awakes and it seems to him "that he had been asleep for a thousand years." This "sleep," of course, takes him back in time, not forward, and so he sees "grey mists," and around him "men in corpse-like hues" with "limbs . . . pulseless and dead." If every epic hero must visit hell, then, for Henry, being in the middle of the group is just that: he sees "the hall of the forest as a charnel place. He believed for an instant that he was in the house of the dead."

If the group influence which Henry has resisted and over which he has gained some dominance causes the individual to see less than he is able, the Homeric view of man purports to allow the individual to "see" more than he actually can. Crane renders the Homeric view meaningless by showing that it too is clouded. That is, if Wilson, the group hero, is given "new eyes" and now apparently sees himself as a "wee thing," then Henry, the Homeric hero, becomes so caught up in his individual desires that his eyes are reduced to "a glazed vacancy." He becomes a "barbarian, a beast." He sees himself as a "pagan who defends his religion," and he sees his battle-rage as "fine, wild, and in some ways, easy. He had been a tremendous figure, no doubt.

By this struggle he had overcome obstacles which he had admitted to be mountains. They had fallen like paper peaks, and he was now what he called a hero."

The whole of chapter 17 describes Henry as being in the grip of the blind battle-rage of Homeric heroes. He forgets that he is merely a private engaged in a small charge on one day of one battle. He thinks of himself as colossal in size and of the other soldiers as "flies sucking insolently at his blood." Although his neck is "bronzed" and he fires his rifle with a fierce grunt as if he were "dealing a blow of the fist with all his strength," he is essentially what one soldier calls this "war devil": "Yeh infernal fool." Heroic Henry certainly is, even in a traditional way, but a bit foolish as well.

Henry soon gains a truer vision. Going with Wilson to get some water, Henry, as well as his image of himself as a Homeric hero, is deflated by a "jangling general" who refers to Henry's regiment, and implicitly to Henry himself, as a lot of "mule drivers." Henry, who had earlier viewed nature as a sympathetic goddess in language filled with Virgilian pathetic fallacy and Christian symbolism (the forest-chapel, for example), and later as a capricious, sometimes malevolent beast much as Homer saw it, now has "new eyes" and sees himself as "very insignificant." This is not necessarily a Christian sense of insignificance, nor even a completely naturalistic one, but simply a realization that compared with more powerful forces, including the regiment, he is powerless. Moreover, since officers are often associated with gods, the sun, and other natural and supernatural entities, Henry's discovery can be seen as developing from his earlier views of nature.

After discovering his insignificance, Henry is in a position to receive a new heroism, a new vision, a "real" vision. In his charge across the field on the second day of battle, it "seemed to the youth that he saw everything":

> Each blade of the green grass was bold and clear. He thought that he was aware of every change in the thin, transparent vapor that floated idly in sheets. The brown or gray trunks of the trees showed each roughness of their surfaces. And the men of the regiment, with their starting eyes and sweating faces, running madly, or falling, as if thrown headlong, to queer, heaped up corpses—all were comprehended. His mind took a mechanical but firm impression, so that afterward everything was pictured and explained to him, save why he himself was there.

A "mechanical" impression of some blades of grass, tree trunks, and sweating, frightened, dying men: that is all one can ever hope to see. The process of epic has been reversed. Virgil had expanded Homer's view of ten or twenty years of glory on the plains before a small town in Asia Minor to include a long-lived empire encompassing the known world. Similarly, the Christian epic of Charlemagne and the crusades are described as world wars. Milton extended the epics beyond human time and farther out than human space. Crane doubled back upon the epic tradition, gradually narrowing space until the epic vision includes only a minute perception and compressing time until that perception exists only for a fleeting instant. It is epical in its achievement and heroic only because Crane has shown it to be the only vision possible for man that remains "bold and clear."

Tiny but unobscured by the smoke of the group or the blinding *menos* of *areté*, Henry's vision has made him Crane's version of the best epic hero. Trying to "observe everything" in his first battle, but failing to "avoid trees and branches," Henry now sees only *something*. Gone is the Roman vision of national destiny and the Miltonic perception of a Puritan God's universe. Heroism is defined in *The Red Badge* as one man's limited but perhaps illusionless vision: grass blades, tree trunks, dying men.

This vision has dominated the literature of the twentieth century and has allowed writers who followed Crane to make the first tentative steps toward a new supreme fiction based upon consciousness of a materialistic universe while discarding the old fictions based upon the imagination. It is upon this vision that Wallace Stevens, for example, built his poetic edifice, and it is because of the new tradition inaugurated by *The Red Badge* that Stevens could write that "in the presence of the violent reality of war, consciousness takes the place of the imagination." This is precisely what happens in this novel.

The epic of consciousness in *The Red Badge* is clearly set forth. Henry begins the novel in his hut, emblem of the enclosed violence of his mind. In this enclosure, cluttered by cracker boxes, clothing, and utensils, he gives vent to his cluttered and conflicting fears and anxieties. "Convicted by himself of many shameful crimes against the gods of tradition" and feeling "alone in space," he has "visions of a thousand tongued fear," and admits that "he would not be able to cope with this monster." When he first goes into combat, he sees "that it would be impossible for him to escape from the regiment. It enclosed him. And there were iron laws of tradition and laws on four sides. He was in a moving box." After escaping from the regimental enclosure, he enters a succession of archetypes for the unconscious—the forest, a swamp, "deep thickets" —each enclosing those which follow, until he reaches "a place where the high, arching boughs made a chapel." Here is a different sort of cave, for this is not at first the enclosure of unconscious fears, nor an enclosure of transcendence, but rather a false cave, like the den of Error (book 1, canto 1) and the cave of Mammon (book 2, canto 7) in the *Faerie Queene,* where the hero is lured toward a false transcendence. In Henry's case the promise

comes in the form of religious transcendentalism. While the insects are pray-
ing and the trees are whispering, Henry pushes open the "green doors" and
enters the chapel. In a paragraph or two Crane both anticipates W. W. Hudson
and Edgar Rice Burroughs and parodies the Schianatulander and chapel scenes
of *Parzival*, for Henry has no sooner entered and is standing "near the
threshold," when "he stopped horror-stricken at the sight of the thing."

> He was being looked at by a dead man who was seated with his
> back against a column-like tree. The corpse was dressed in a
> uniform that once had been blue but now was faded to a melan-
> choly shade of green. The eyes, staring at the youth, had changed
> to the dull hue to be seen on the side of a dead fish. The mouth
> was opened. Its red had changed to an appalling yellow. Over the
> grey skin of the face ran little ants. One was trundling some sort
> of a bundle along the upper lip.

The stark clarity of this paragraph, with its excruciatingly painful materialism,
provides a perfect contrast to the "religious half-light" leading up to this
description. While the description is faintly reminiscent of Thoreau's mock
epic paragraphs on ants in *Walden*, its main purpose seems to be to pose
starkly the problem that Henry and other epic heroes must face. Somehow,
the pathetic fallacy, the religious rose-colored glasses, must be removed, and
Henry must still be able to face the "thing" —the fact of death. At this early
stage, the contrast is too great for Henry and he responds by screaming and
fleeing from the enclosure, which promised transcendence but delivered only
death. Another way of saying it is that he was lulled by the imagination and
then confronted by pure consciousness. He heads back to the regiment. Only
later, after facing death in the field, does Henry accept a classical, almost
Lucretian materialism with respect to mortality. This seems to be what Henry
learns: "He knew that he would no more quail before his guides wherever
they should point. He had been to touch the great death and found that, after
all, it was but the great death."

Before this, however, Henry has other caves to face. It may be said that
after he crosses the river in chapter 3, Henry is subterranean for nearly the
remainder of the novel, much as Dante is throughout the *Inferno*. The others
are merely caves within caves, hells within Hades. One of these is the night
camp of the regiment in chapter 13. Here Henry catches "glimpses of visages
that loomed pallid and ghostly, lit with a phosphorescent glow." Another
enclosure of failed transcendence, this camp is like that to which the captain
brings the reluctant voyagers. This too contains a window on the stars: "Far
off to the right, through a window in the forest could be seen a handful of

stars." Managing to resist the temptations of even this "charnel house," Henry subsequently overcomes the numerous enclosures formed by the smoke of the regiment's many rifles and achieves his "bold and clear" vision.

DEFEATS

The latest episode in the long controversy about the quality of *The Red Badge* begins with Henry Binder's 1978 articles and 1979 edition of Crane's novel for *The Norton Anthology of American Literature*—articles in which he proposes restoring, and an edition in which he does restore, several manuscript passages to the printed text. Restoring these passages, Binder claims, makes a muddled novel clear and consistent. The controversy regarding whether or not Henry "grows" is resolved: he does not; the novel is clearly ironic. While agreeing that the original Appleton edition poses problems, Donald Pizer contends that the traditional text is the best we have until evidence stronger than Binder's appears. Pizer takes issue with Binder on essentially two points: first, that because there is no evidence suggesting that Crane was pressured into making the cuts, it can only be assumed that he freely chose to make them; and second, that Binder errs in assuming that "a clear and consistent novel is better than an ambivalent and ambiguous one."

Because it involves an entire chapter, the longest of Binder's additions must be addressed in some detail by anyone discussing the structure of *The Red Badge*. This is especially true of a discussion of classical epic structure, where arithmetical divisions are significant and the notion of a twenty-five-chapter epic poses some problems. The restored chapter is the original manuscript's chapter 12, coming after the Appleton chapter 11. Traditional epics are structurally divided in half. A twenty-five-chapter novel based on epic would be divided somewhere near the middle of chapter 13, leaving twelve and a half chapters on either side. Chapter 13 in the new Norton edition is chapter 12 of the traditional Appleton edition. The middle of this chapter describes Henry receiving his wound, a description already discussed as pivotal to the work. Since Henry is in no position to do much on his own between the time he is wounded (the middle of the Norton) and the time the cheery man deposits him with the regiment (ending the traditional text's first half), the different editions have little effect on the validity of the novel's epic structure.

The content of the added chapter does little more than reaffirm the metronomic quality of Henry's thoughts and emotions as they move between extremes of Nietzschean egotism and Paulean self-flagellation. On one hand, "it was always clear to the youth that he was entirely different from other men; that his mind had been cast in a unique mold. Hence laws that might be just to ordinary men, were, when applied to him, peculiar and galling outrages. On the other hand, when "his mind pictured the death of Jim Conklin" and in it "he saw the shadows of his fate," he felt himself to be "unfit": "He did not come into the scheme of further life. His tiny part had been played and he must go."

The additions appearing in the 1979 Norton edition of *The Red Badge* do little to enhance or diminish the notion of the *The Red Badge* as having structural and thematic roots in classical epic. At the same time, since the passages do little more than reaffirm the greatness of *The Red Badge,* the classical dicta of economy and simplicity ought to apply, and one giving a supposedly classical reading of a work ought to side with his sources.

The final chapter of *The Red Badge* presents perhaps the greatest critical problems in the Crane canon. Many of the critical reservations about Crane's importance and abilities rest in the complexities and supposed inconsistencies (even inanities) of this chapter.

The last chapter is both complete and consistent. It is a deliberate reversal of all that has gone before. Throughout the largest portion of *The Red Badge,* Henry is in the process of sloughing off both the Christian-group "walking-sticks" of Stallman's interpretation and the Homeric "creeds" of this reading. If the final chapter of *The Red Badge* is naturalistic, it is so only within the context of Crane's conception of the epic.

That a man may learn and then forget, as Holton says, pervades Crane's writings; in terms of the epic nature of *The Red Badge,* a man may forget and then remember. In the first twenty-three chapters, Henry proceeds to "forget" all previous cultural notions and epic concepts about the way life is. Having "forgotten," he finally achieves an impressionistic vision of the individual man unencumbered by epic and cultural trappings. In the final chapter, however, Henry "remembers"; his former epic value systems sweep back over him, and he is left at the end dreaming dreams he had dreamt in the beginning.

Throughout twenty-three chapters of the novel the major concern is to discover the true nature of heroism. In the final chapter, however, all epic values are specifically refuted. Because he forgets the vision that he has found, and the limited heroism he has discovered, Henry becomes a nonhero. *The Red Badge,* too, is negated, a nonepic. Unlike Milton, Virgil, and Homer, Crane does not wait for his particular notion of heroism to be satirized by others; he mocks it himself.

The Red Badge of Courage ends by mocking the epic genre and its heroic ideals. But the novel, so saturated with epic tradition, cannot be exiled from the epic province. Its exploitation of epic conventions attests to the lingering vitality of the genre, but its annihilation of heroism—Homeric, Virgilian, Catholic, or Miltonic—at the same time exposes the genre's vulnerability. The novel marks a transition from the formal epic tradition to all that is Homerically nonepic in modern fiction: triumphant chaos and successful deceit.

The last chapter is an ironic recapitulation of each epic value system present in the remainder of the book. Homeric *arete* is savagely mocked, as is Christian-group heroism. The primary target, however, is that final concept of heroism, Crane's own, which Henry has achieved earlier: that concept based only on the individual's ability to peer into the pit of reality with a gaze unclouded by cultural and epic notions of what the world is like. Throughout this final chapter, Henry's (and Crane's) perception-based, impressionistic heroism is mocked by means of an ironic significance attached to images of and references to the sense of sight. Henry enters the chapter a cleareyed hero; he exits blind and deluded.

As the chapter opens, the battle has begun to wane and the sounds of war have begun "to grow intermittent and weaker." Henry's newfound vision soon runs the gamut of perception from egotistical pride to cringing guilt and humility, and is, in effect, also becoming "weaker." As the regiment begins to "retrace its way" like a snake "winding off in the direction of the river," Henry is with it, recrossing the Stygian stream he had crossed in chapter 3. Similarly, Henry's mind is "undergoing a subtle change": "It took moments for it to cast off its battleful ways and resume its accustomed course of thought. Gradually his brain emerged from the clogged clouds and at last he was enabled to more closely comprehend himself and his circumstance." After "his first thoughts were given to rejoicings" because he had "escaped" the battle, Henry's vision becomes distorted. First, he contemplates his "achievements." With Homeric eyes he sees his deeds as "great and shining." His deluded vision is so distorted that he dresses those deeds in the royal "wide purple and gold," which, on Henry, give off sparkles "of various deflections."

Next, he assumes Christian eyes, and his visions of Homeric glory, of *areté*, are destroyed by an exaggerated guilt brought on by the memory of his crime against the tattered man. The tattered man had tormented him unmercifully, but all Henry sees is a grotesquely distorted image of the gentle tattered man transmogrified into a weird Christian version of some apostle of revenge who visits on Henry a "vision of cruelty." One delusion displaces another, so that Henry's previous vision, as well as his heroism, becomes changed and meaningless, because no longer is it his alone. Homeric pride makes Henry a strutting fool, and Christian-group guilt betrays him as a coward.

Images of and references to vision provide further ironic commentary on the quality of "perception" inherent in the two traditional epic value systems. For example, Crane mocks three specific aspects of *areté* in the final chapter by proving them to be false or wildly exaggerated visions of reality. He first mocks the lack of any firm moral sense in the ancient Greek battle code. At times, Henry has done less than his *areté* demands of him, but he rightly ignores this when contemplating his great deeds and he even feels "gleeful and unregretting." Another aspect of *areté* mocked by Crane is the all-important result of the Homeric hero's desire for glory, "public recognition of his *areté*: it runs through Greek life. Henry tends to exaggerate the quality of his *areté*, and consequently the recognition it deserves, in a sort of daydream vision, a "procession of memory" in which "his public deeds were paraded in great and shining prominence." The final mockery concerns that aspect of heroism lying at the heart of *areté*: the recognition of the hero's superiority over his peers. If we remember the soldier's comic, even ridiculous speech concerning "Flem's" bravery and the somewhat qualifying and dubiously conferred title "jimhickey," Henry's recollections seem to be all out of proportion: "He recalled with a thrill of joy the respectful comments of his fellows upon his conduct."

Henry's progression toward heroism during the first twenty-three chapters reverses and inverts itself in the last chapter, for Henry's vision is a distortion that destroys his notion of Homeric bravery and of *areté*. Henry's semi-sin of leaving the tattered man haunts him. Crane here employs a parody of nineteenth-century Protestant tracts, much as he has described Henry's Homeric deeds in the language traditionally used to depict the victory marches of great warriors: "A spectre of reproach came to him. There loomed the dogging memory of the tattered soldier—he who gored by bullets and faint for blood, had fretted concerning an imagined wound in another; he who had loaned his last of strength and intellect for the tall soldier; he who, blind with weariness and pain, had been deserted in the field." Henry is then "followed" by a "vision of cruelty" which clings "near to him always" and darkens "his view of these deeds in purple and gold." This "somber phantom" heightens Henry's guilt; he becomes "afraid it would stand before him all his life." Thus, "he saw his vivid error." After recognizing that he had sinned, Henry receives partial expiation in the form of partial forgetfulness: "Yet he gradually mustered force to put the sin at a distance. And at last his eyes seemed to open to some new ways. He found that he could now look back upon the brass and bombast of his earlier gospels and see them truly. He was gleeful when he discovered that he now despised them." Henry here exchanges one false view of himself for another. The Homeric vision has given way to a Christian-group one. Crane, with beautiful, lyric irony, moves Henry away from the war and from the battle in his mind: "So it came to pass that as he trudged from the place of blood and wrath his soul changed." Henry now believes that "the world was a world for him," as a Christian-group hero should.

There is yet another way, however, in which Crane sets about to destroy the epic. By ironically disparaging the epic view of man's history, Crane ridicules the concept that readers have of the epic genre. The epic has long been one of the more revered forms of historical interpretation and cultural expression. Through epic poetry Homer presents man as a godlike animal struggling to gain a measure of immortality through the public recognition of great deeds. But the Homeric man was like Lear in the storm—alone, naked, and "unaccommodated" —and this is probably why Crane preferred this view more than other traditional views: it was closer to his notion, expressed in "The Blue Hotel," that "conceit is the very engine of life." Virgil gave man more hope by giving him the opportunity to identify and merge with the immortality of a national group. By interpreting history in terms of a great empire, he was also in some measure espousing a kind of immortality. Medieval and Renaissance epic, including *The Song of Roland* and Tasso's *Gerusalemme liberata,* glorified the church militant, ordained to victory. Milton went even farther. He regarded man as completely unworthy of immortality, but acknowledged man's hope in a merciful God's love; man's earthly history spans the interval between creation and final redemption.

Crane felt that these interpretations of history were, to one degree or another, part of a giant hoax willfully perpetuated on man by man. At times he could be downright Aeschylean: "Hope," as Berryman quotes him, " is the most vacuous emotion of mankind."

The Red Badge is a denial of the epic view of history, which Crane felt creates an absurd, illusory, and vacuous emotion.

In the first twenty-three chapters of *The Red Badge* an epic fable is presented which carries the reader back through history. Henry begins *in medias res*, confused and torn between the two major epic views of history, and between two epic value systems as they have filtered through the epic into and out of culture. One of Henry's great accomplishments is his success in throwing off, if only for a short time, the Christian-group view that has dominated the long history of the social epic—indeed of all intellectual life in the West. Next, Henry rejects the rest of history, as recorded by the individual epic, by sloughing off the hope of being an immortal, Homeric "war devil." Finally, past all Christian doctrine, beyond the emotional slither of patriotism and breast-beating brass and bombast, this young man finds a vision in some blades of grass and the grooved bark of a few trees. He is, for an instant, free as few have ever been free; he is loosed from the illusions of history. Perhaps, because it is so limited in duration, Crane is mocking his own illusion, and that of Americans from Franklin to Ginsberg, that man can indeed throw off the process of history and the illusions it etches into the brain.

However, those twenty-three chapters may not be a fairy-tale epic. Crane may have felt that through catalytic and catastrophic experiences like war, man can scrape the scales of history from his eyes. Perhaps all the teachings of history are reduced to absurdity in the midst of the immense experience, if one tries hard enough to see for himself. Perhaps one can universalize Crane's statement that "a man is only responsible for the personal quality of his honesty" of vision. "A man is sure to fail at it," he said, "but there is something in the failure." Although the paucity of the vision may make it ironic, there is some heroism involved in the sheer ability to perceive reality. In either case, however, the last chapter of the novel indicates that Crane felt heroism to be impossible beyond the immediacy of experience.

This aspect of the last chapter functions by way of a metaphorical equation: memory is to the individual as history is to the species. As Henry moves away from the immediate experience, his memory creates lies and delusions about that experience. The ironic laughter from Crane results from his belief that man cannot really learn from experience, even when he can reach an illusionless view of reality through that experience. Once it is over, once one is no longer staring at the face of red death, then memory, or history, distorts that experience all out of any recognizable proportion.

In the last chapter, history becomes what memory becomes—a mechanism for man to build his self-image. Through the two main thrusts of the history of Western civilization, as expressed by the epic genre, man is deluded into believing himself to be either more or less than he actually is. In the end, Henry is led by his memory to believe with conviction all the mad, distorted hopes of epic history. Ironically, "at last his eyes opened on some new ways." These are new ways only for Henry; they are as old as history. Darwin mounted on Mather.

These "new ways" are a collation of Homeric and Christian-group values. There is still much pride in Henry, but also much humility. Together, they form a paradoxically proud humility: "He felt a quiet man-hood, non-assertive but of sturdy and strong blood." The sum of Henry's wisdom, apparently gained from these seemingly "new" ways, and required of epic heroes, is expressed in what becomes, upon close examination, a meaningless platitude worthy of the climax of a dime-novel adventure: "He had been to touch the great death, and found that, after all, it was but the great death. He was a man."

The final delusion of history and memory Crane repudiated is that of "hope." Part of the reason that Virgil and Milton wrote epics was to give men hope. Beautifully parodic, and powerfully ironic, the last paragraphs of *The Red Badge* express the hopes of Aeneas and Adam, of Columbus and Hiawatha, and of people at all times and in all places, hot to cool, hard to soft, pain to pleasure, hell to heaven:

> So it came to pass that as he trudged from the place of blood and wrath, his soul changed. He had come from hot-ploughshares to prospects of clover tranquility and it was as if hot-ploughshares were not. Scars faded as flowers.
>
> It rained. The procession of weary soldiers became a bedraggled train, despondent and muttering, marching with churning effort, in a trough of liquid brown mud under a low, wretched sky. Yet the youth smiled, for he saw that the world was a world for him though many discovered it to be made of oaths and walking-sticks. . . . The sultry nightmare was in the past. He had been an animal blistered and sweating in the heat and pain of war. He turned now with a lover's thirst, to images of tranquil skies, fresh meadows, cool brooks; an existence of soft and eternal peace.

No one lives a life of "soft and eternal peace," except in deluded dreams, and Crane knew it. "He was almost illusionless," Berryman said of Crane, "whether about his subjects or himself. Perhaps his only illusion was the heroic one; and not even this . . . escaped his irony."

MICHAEL   FRIED

Stephen Crane's Upturned Faces

In a well-known passage early on in *The Red Badge of Courage,* Henry Fleming (whom the narrative mainly refers to as "the youth") encounters the first
of several corpses that turn up in the novel:

> Once the line encountered the body of a dead soldier. He lay upon
> his back staring at the sky. He was dressed in an awkward suit
> of yellowish brown. The youth could see that the soles of his shoes
> had been worn to the thinness of writing paper, and from a great
> rent in one the dead foot projected piteously. And it was as if fate
> had betrayed the soldier. In death it exposed to his enemies that
> poverty which in life he had perhaps concealed from his friends.
>
> The ranks opened covertly to avoid the corpse. The invulnerable
> dead man forced a way for himself. The youth looked keenly at
> the ashen face. The wind raised the tawny beard. It moved as if
> a hand were stroking it. He vaguely desired to walk around and
> around the body and stare; the impulse of the living to try to read
> in dead eyes the answer to the Question.

All of Stephen Crane's formidable powers of defamiliarization are quietly at
work in this passage. The corpse is inert but active, betrayed and poverty-
stricken but also invulnerable and forcing, avoided by the ranks of living men,
which we imagine parting to give it a certain berth, and yet its tawny beard
is manipulated by the wind in a gesture of extraordinary intimacy that more

This essay as it appears here is the first part of chapter 2 in Michael Fried's forthcoming book, *Realism, Writing, Disfiguration: On Thomas Eakins and Stephen Crane.*
© 1987 by The University of Chicago, Press University Press, 1987.

145

than anything else establishes the dead soldier's uncanniness for us. As for Henry Fleming's relation to the corpse, it is at once apparently straightforward, as when we are told that the youth could see the soles of the dead man's shoes or that he looked keenly at the dead man's face, and conspicuously indeterminate, as when Crane's prose formulates thoughts that could not possibly be those of his protagonist ("And it was as if fate had betrayed the soldier.") but seem nevertheless to follow from the latter's perceptions. Indeed the apparent straightforwardness itself has disconcerting aspects. Thus the succession of grammatically simple sentences in the second paragraph ("The youth looked keenly at the ashen face. The wind raised the tawny beard. It moved as if a hand were stroking it.") seems almost to imply causal relationship, as if the youth were acting on the corpse through the medium of the wind, though characteristically the next sentence (beginning "He vaguely desired to walk around and around the body and stare") comes close to dissolving the distinction between living and dead both by virtue of the ambiguity of the initial pronoun and because staring is precisely the action attributed to the corpse in the second sentence of the first paragraph. It is as though throughout the passage the separateness of the youth both from the corpse and from the narrator is palpably the accomplishment of *absolutely* local effects of writing, which here as elsewhere in *The Red Badge* suggests that we may be in the neighborhood of a "sublime" scenario of fantasized aggression, identification, and differentiation not unlike the one that partly governs the painter's relation to key personages in *The Gross Clinic* [painting by Thomas Eakins].

But my aim in citing this passage is not to insist on that affinity. Instead I want to emphasize, first, the salience in both paragraphs of a particular bodily position, that of the corpse lying flat on its back (this is what allows the wind to get at the beard); second, the characterization of the corpse's upward-staring face as an object of another character's keen attention and the related fact that something, in this case something seemingly gentle, is done to the face or at least to a metonym for it (the tawny beard); and third, the dramatization, through the image of the protruding foot, of an unexpected detail—that the soles of the dead soldier's shoes "had been worn to the thinness of writing paper." I won't try to gloss these matters here but will move directly on to another passage in Crane, this one from his novella "The Monster."

The passage is taken from an astonishing scene in which the Negro Henry Johnson, who works for the Trescott family as a coachman, goes heroically into a burning house in order to save young Jimmie Trescott from certain death. Johnson rushes up the stairs and finds Jimmie having just awakened in his own room, but when he tries to carry the boy down he discovers that flames and smoke have made the route impassable. For a moment he despairs, then recalls a private staircase leading from another bedroom to an apartment that Jimmie's father, a doctor, had fitted up as a laboratory. But when Johnson finally makes his way there he discovers not only that that room too is on fire but that the doctor's chemicals are exploding in fantastic hues and forms ("At the entrance to the laboratory he confronted a strange spectacle. The room was like a garden in the region where might be burning flowers. Flames of violet, crimson, green, blue, orange, and purple were blooming everywhere. There was one blaze that was precisely the hue of a delicate coral. In another place was a mass that lay merely in phosphorescent inaction like a pile of emeralds. But all these marvels were to be seen dimly through clouds of heaving, turning, deadly smoke"). After pausing on the threshold, Johnson rushes across the room with the boy still in his arms; just then an explosion occurs and "a delicate, trembling sapphire shape like a fairy lady" blocks his path; Johnson tries to duck past her but she is "swifter than eagles" and her talons are said to catch in him as he does so. Whereupon, "Johnson lurched forward, twisting this way and that way, rolled to the edge of the floor and beneath the window." (Jimmie will later be saved.) The scene concludes:

> Johnson had fallen with his head at the base of an old-fashioned desk. There was a row of jars upon the top of this desk. For the most part, they were silent amid this rioting, but there was one which seemed to hold a scintillant and writhing serpent.
>
> Suddenly the glass splintered, and a ruby-red snakelike thing poured its thick length out upon the top of the old desk. It coiled and hesitated, and then began to swim a languorous way down the mahogany slant. At the angle it waved its sizzling molten head to and fro over the closed eyes of the man beneath it. Then, in a moment, with mystic impulse, it moved again, and the red snake flowed directly down into Johnson's upturned face.
>
> Afterward the trail of this creature seemed to reek, and amid flames and low explosions drops like red-hot jewels pattered softly down it at leisurely intervals.

By the end of this passage we again are presented with an unmoving body lying face up on the ground. In this case the body is not that of a corpse and its eyes are closed rather than open; but the extent of the author's, or say the novella's, investment in the body's final position becomes plain when we consider the oddly unpersuasive account of the lurchings and twistings that produce it. Another difference from the description of the corpse in *The Red Badge* is that no second character is represented gazing at Johnson's upturned face. But the passage from the "The Monster" narrates the destruction of Johnson's face (we are soon told that "he now had no face. His face had simply been burned away," and the remainder of the plot will turn on the dreadfulness to sight of the nonface with which he has been left (although never described, it gives rise to horrendous consequences whenever it is glimpsed). Maybe too the sheer gorgeousness of the color imagery of the burning laboratory should be read in part as a displacement of effects of seeing that the logic of the narrative doesn't allow the scene to represent directly (the "sapphire shape like a fairy lady" comes closest to being a possible agent of vision). In any event, something is done to Johnson's face, and this time what is done is far from gentle. Finally, in light of the comparison of the soles of the dead man's shoes to writing paper in the excerpt from *The Red Badge,* I am struck by the fact that Johnson ends up lying "with his head at the base of an old-fashioned desk," a piece of furniture that one inevitably connects with the activity of writing; and just in case this seems to be making too much of an incidental detail, I shall quote again the sentence that immediately precedes the account of Johnson's appalling disfiguration, but with two key verbs italicized: "For the most part, they [the jars on the desk] were silent amid this *rioting,* but there was one which seemed to hold a scintillant and *writhing* serpent." "Whether or not we understand the particular jar to contain ink, the verbs in question evoke a third verb, *writing,* that comes close to rhyming, audially and visually, with the other two. (Later in this essay I shall argue that the images of serpents and fire that turn up frequently in Crane's texts belong essentially to a metaphorics of writing.)

The third text by Crane I want to consider is the late short tale "The Upturned Face"; in effect it takes the motifs and preoccupations I have identified in the passages from *The Red Badge* and "The Monster" and constructs around them a brief, two-part narrative of tremendous force and uncertain significance. What ostensibly is narrated is the burial, under enemy fire, of a dead officer by two fellow officers who had served with him for years. The opening paragraphs read as follows:

> "What will we do now?" said the adjutant, troubled and excited.
> "Bury him," said Timothy Lean.
> The two officers looked down close to their toes where lay the body of their comrade. The face was chalk-blue; gleaming eyes stared at the sky. Over the two upright figures was a windy sound of bullets, and on the top of the hill, Lean's prostrate company of Spitzbergen infantry was firing measured volleys.

Two men from the company are assigned to dig a grave and Lean and the adjutant proceed to search the corpse's clothes for "things" (as the adjutant puts it). Lean hesitates to touch the first bloodstained button on the dead man's tunic but at last completes the search and rises "with a ghastly face. He had gathered a watch, a whistle, a pipe, a tobacco pouch, a handkerchief, a little case of cards and papers." Meanwhile the bullets keep spitting overhead and the two lower ranks labor at digging the grave; their completion of the task is announced in the following short paragraph:

> The grave was finished. It was not a masterpiece—poor little shallow thing. Lean and the adjutant again looked at each other in a curious silent communication.

The two officers proceed to tumble the dead man into the grave, taking care not to feel his body as they do so; after saying a mangled prayer (based, it would seem, on the service for the dead at sea) they are ready to oversee the covering up of his remains. At this point, the first paragraph of the second part of the narrative, the motif of the upturned face returns with new force:

> One of the aggrieved privates came forward with his shovel. He lifted his first shovel load of earth and for a moment of inexplicable hesitation it was held poised above this corpse which from its chalk-blue face looked keenly out from the grave. Then the soldier emptied his shovel on—on the feet.
>
> Timothy Lean felt as if tons had been swiftly lifted from off his forehead. He had felt that perhaps the private might empty the shovel on—on the face. It had been emptied on the feet. There was a great point gained there—ha, ha!—the first shovelful had been emptied on the feet. How satisfactory!

Suddenly the man with the shovel is struck by a bullet in the left arm and Lean seizes the shovel and begins to fill the grave himself; as the dirt lands it makes a sound— "plop." The adjutant suggests that it might have been better not to try to bury the body just at that time, but Lean rudely tells him to shut his mouth and persists at his task. The tale concludes:

> Soon there was nothing to be seen but the chalk-blue face. Lean filled the shovel. . . . "Good God," he cried to the adjutant. "Why didn't you turn him somehow when you put him in? This— " Then Lean began to stutter.
>
> The adjutant understood. He was pale to the lips. "Go on, man," he cried, beseechingly, almost in a shout. . . . Lean swung back the

shovel; it went forward in a pendulum curve. When the earth
landed it made a sound—plop. (Crane's ellipses)

Much of the cumulative effect of "The Upturned Face" has been lost in
my summary, but even so several points are clear. First, once more we find
at the center of the scene a dead man lying on his back staring upward; in
fact, as I have noted, we are presented with such a figure twice over, at the
opening of the tale, where it is described as lying at the feet of Lean and the
adjutant, and at the beginning of the second part, as the first shovelful of
dirt is held suspended above it. Second, the corpse's chalk-blue upturned face
is on both occasions the principal object of Lean's and the adjutant's attention, and once again something uncanny and in a strong sense disfiguring
happens to that face—in fact the entire second part of the tale turns on Lean's
repugnance at the prospect of having to cover the dead man's face with dirt.
(The exact degree of violence this implies seems to fall somewhere between
the scenes from *The Red Badge* and "The Monster.") And third, although
a thematics of writing is no more than hinted at by the recurrent epithet "chalk-
blue" and perhaps also by the little case of cards and papers that Lean removes
from the dead man, the newly excavated and still empty grave is characterized, indeed is half-addressed, as "not a masterpiece—poor little shallow
thing," a phrase that, however ironically, deploys a vocabulary of artistic valua-
tion that one can imagine the author applying (again ironically: Crane seems
to have thought especially well of this tale) to "The Upturned Face" itself.
I suggest too that the ostensible action of the tale—the digging of a grave,
the tumbling of a corpse into its shallow depths, and then the covering of
the corpse and specifically its upturned face with shovelfuls of dirt—and the
movement of the prose of its telling are meant as nearly as possible to coin-
cide, as if each were ultimately a figure for the other: this is one reason why,
for example, the text comes to an end with the quasi-word "plop," which is
nothing more nor less than the verbal representation of the sound made when
the last shovelful of dirt falls on the grave, or if not the very last at any rate
the one that covers the chalk-blue face once and for all. That the protagonist's
name, Timothy Lean, invites being read as a barely disguised version of the
author's reinforces this suggestion, all the more so in that the adjutant remains
nameless and the dead man is referred to only once, by Lean, as "old Bill."
All this is to read "The Upturned Face" as representing, and in a sense enact-
ing, the writing of "The Upturned Face," which as a general proposition about
a literary work is today pretty much standard fare. What is interesting to consider, however, is why this particular text lends itself so fully to such a reading,
or to broaden our discussion to include the passages from *The Red Badge*

and "The Monster," what it means that motifs of an upturned face and the disfiguring of that face are in all three cases conjoined with a thematization or, in "The Upturned Face" itself, a sustained if displaced representation of the act of writing.

Here is 'a partial answer. Just as in [Rembrandt] Peale's *Graphics* a primitive ontological difference between the allegedly upright or erect "space" of reality and the horizontal "space" of writing/drawing emerged as problematic for the graphic enterprise, and just as in Eakins's art an analogous difference between the horizontal "space" of writing/drawing and the vertical or upright "space" of painting turned out to play a crucial role with respect both to choice of subject matter and to all that is traditionally comprised under the notion of style, so in the production of these paradigmatic texts by Crane an implicit contrast between the respective "spaces" of reality and of literary representation—of writing (and in a sense, as we shall see, of writing/drawing)—required that a human character, ordinarily upright and so to speak forward-looking, be rendered horizontal and upward-facing so as to match the horizontality and upward-facingness of the blank page on which the action of inscription was taking place. Understood in these terms, Crane's upturned faces are at once synecdoches for the bodies of those characters and singularly concentrated metaphors for the sheets of writing paper that the author had before him, as is spelled out, by means of a displacement from one end of the body to the other, by the surprising description of the worn-down soles of the dead soldier's shoes in the passage from *The Red Badge*. (The displacement is retroactively signaled by the allusion to reading in the last sentence of the second paragraph.)

Thus for example the size and proportions of a human face and that of an ordinary piece of writing paper are roughly comparable. An original coloristic disfiguration of all three faces, either by death making one ashen and another chalk-blue or simply by Henry Johnson's blackness, may be taken as evoking the special blankness of the as yet unwritten page. (A preparatory blankness is associated with Johnson's face—actually with his facelessness—in a scene in Reifsnyder's barber shop; the crucial passage reads: "As the barber foamed the lather on the cheeks of the engineer he seemed to be thinking heavily. Then suddenly he burst out. 'How would you like to be with no face?' he cried to the assemblage.") And their further disfiguration, by the wind that is said to have raised the soldier's tawny beard (in this context the verb betrays more aggressive connotations than at first declare themselves), by the ruby-red snakelike thing that flows down into the unconscious Johnson's visage, and by the shovelful of dirt that Lean agonizingly deposits on the last visible portion of his dead comrade, defines the enterprise of writing—of inscribing and thereby in effect covering the blank page with text—as an "unnatural" process that undoes but also complements an equally or already "unnatural" state of affairs. (It goes without saying that the text in question is invariably organized in *lines* of writing, a noun that occurs, both in plural and singular form, with surprising frequency in Crane's prose, as for example in the sentence, "Once the line encountered the body of a dead soldier.") In fact one way of glossing the tumbling of the body into the newly dug grave in "The Upturned Face" is an acknowledgment that the upward-facingness of the corpse, hence of the page, is not so much a brute given as a kind of artifact— not precisely the result of conscious choice (Lean and the adjutant don't try to arrange the corpse face up) but by the same token not the issue of inhuman necessity (before a word has been written on it, the blank page tells a story of agency).

What remains obscure, however, is why in the passages we have examined the act of writing is thematized as *violent* disfigurement and, especially in those from "The Monster" and "The Upturned Face," why it is associated with effects of horror and repugnance—as though writing for Crane, like painting for Eakins, were in essential respects an excruciating enterprise. Nor does anything I have said begin to answer the broader question of what it means that figures of the blank page and of the action or process of writing play an important role in three of Crane's greatest works.

Chronology

1871	Stephen Crane born November 1 in Newark, New Jersey, youngest child of Jonathan Townley Crane, a Methodist minister, and Mary Helen Peck Crane.
1874–82	Family moves to Port Jervis, New York, where Crane first attends school. After his father's death in 1880, Crane's mother moves the family to Asbury Park, New Jersey. She writes religious articles for Methodist journals and other newspapers.
1891	Crane attends Syracuse University, where he meets Hamlin Garland. He leaves after his first year and moves to the New York City area. His mother dies.
1892	Crane fails at several newspaper jobs but publishes six Sullivan County sketches.
1893–94	*Maggie: A Girl of the Streets* is printed privately. Crane meets W. D. Howells. He begins work on *The Red Badge of Courage*, *George's Mother*, and a collection of poems.
1895–96	Crane travels to Mexico. Publication of *The Red Badge of Courage* and *The Black Riders* wins him instant fame. He publishes a revision of *Maggie* with *George's Mother*. En route to Cuba, Crane meets Cora Taylor, proprietress of a house of prostitution in Florida.
1897	Crane is shipwrecked off the coast of Florida. He bases "The Open Boat" upon the incident. He travels to Greece with Cora Taylor to cover the Greco-Turkish War. Crane writes "The Monster" and "The Bride Comes to Yellow Sky" and becomes acquainted with Joseph Conrad.
1898	*The Open Boat and Other Tales of Adventure* is published. Crane becomes a correspondent in Cuba during the Spanish-American War.

1899   Crane publishes *War Is Kind*. He resides with Cora at Brede Place in England. He suffers a massive tubercular hemorrhage.

1900   Crane dies of tuberculosis in Badenweiler, Germany, on June 5. *Whilomville Stories, Great Battles of the World*, and *Last Words* appear posthumously. A novel, *The O'Ruddy*, is completed by Robert Barr.

Contributors

HAROLD BLOOM, Sterling Professor of the Humanities at Yale University, is the author of *The Anxiety of Influence, Poetry and Repression,* and many other volumes of literary criticism. His forthcoming study, *Freud: Transference and Authority,* attempts a full-scale reading of all of Freud's major writings. A MacArthur Prize Fellow, he is general editor of five series of literary criticism published by Chelsea House.

JOHN BERRYMAN is widely recognized as one of the finest contemporary American poets. His collections of verse include *77 Dream Songs* and *His Toy His Dream His Rest.* He also published a collection of essays, *The Freedom of the Poet,* in addition to his critical biography of Stephen Crane. A novel, *Recovery,* appeared after his death in 1972.

DANIEL G. HOFFMAN is Professor of English at the University of Pennsylvania. His recent critical works include *Barbarous Knowledge: Myth in the Poetry of Yeats, Graves, and Muir* and *"Moonlight Dries No Mittens": Carl Sandburg Reconsidered.* He is also the author of several volumes of verse, including *Able Was I Ere I Saw Elba* and *Brotherly Love.*

STANLEY WERTHEIM teaches English at William Patterson College, Wayne, New Jersey. He compiled *Hawthorne, Melville, Stephen Crane: A Critical Bibliography.* He has also written study guides to the works of Thomas Wolfe and Sinclair Lewis.

DANIEL WEISS was Professor of Literature at San Francisco State University. He is the author of a psychoanalytic study of D. H. Lawrence, *Oedipus in Nottingham,* and of the posthumously collected essays in *The Critic Agonistes.*

MARSTON LaFRANCE teaches at Carleton University in Ottawa, Canada.

ALAN TRACHTENBERG is Professor of American Studies and English at Yale University. His works include *Brooklyn Bridge: Fact and Symbol* and *The Incorporation of America: Culture and Society in the Gilded Age.* He was awarded fellowships from the Rockefeller Foundation and the Wilson Center to continue a study of photography and American culture.

JAMES NAGEL is Professor of English at Northeastern University. He has edited *Vision and Value: A Thematic Introduction to the Short Story* and a volume of critical essays on *Catch-22*.

HAROLD KAPLAN teaches English at Northwestern University. He is the author of *Democratic Humanism and American Literature.*

CAROL HURD GREEN is Associate Dean of Arts and Sciences at Boston College. Among her works in progress are a study of women in art and politics in the 1960s and a study of the works of Dorothy Day.

CHESTER L. WOLFORD is Professor of English at Behrend College.

MICHAEL FRIED is Professor of Humanities and the History of Art at The Johns Hopkins University, where he is also Director of the Humanities Center. He has written books on Morris Louis and on painting in the age of Diderot, and is currently working on a study of the art of Courbet.

Bibliography

Adams, R. P. "Naturalistic Fiction: 'The Open Boat.'" *Tulane Studies in English* 4 (1954): 137–46.

Ahnebrink, Lars. *The Beginnings of Naturalism in American Fiction: A Study of the Works of Hamlin Garland, Stephen Crane, and Frank Norris.* New York: Russell & Russell, 1961.

Bassan, Maurice, ed. *Stephen Crane: A Collection of Critical Essays.* Englewood Cliffs, N. J.: Prentice-Hall, 1967.

Beer, Thomas. *Stephen Crane: A Study in American Letters.* New York: Knopf, 1923.

Bergon, Frank. *Stephen Crane's Artistry.* New York: Columbia University Press, 1975.

Berryman, John. *Stephen Crane.* New York: Sloane, 1950.

———. "Stephen Crane." In *The Freedom of the Poet,* 168–84. New York: Farrar, Straus & Giroux, 1976.

Berthoff, Warner. *The Ferment of Realism.* New York: Free Press, 1965.

Bridgman, Richard. *The Colloquial Style in America.* New York: Oxford University Press, 1966.

Cady, Edwin H. "Howells and Crane: Violence, Decorum, and Reality." In *The Light of Common Day.* Bloomington: Indiana University Press, 1971.

———. *Stephen Crane.* New York: Twayne, 1962.

———. "Stephen Crane and the Strenuous Life." *ELH* 28 (1961): 376–82.

Cazemajou, Jean. *Stephen Crane.* Minneapolis: University of Minnesota Press, 1969.

Colvert, James. "The Origins of Stephen Crane's Literary Creed." *University of Texas Studies in English* 34 (1955): 179–88.

———. *Stephen Crane.* San Diego: Harcourt Brace Jovanovich, 1984.

Ellison, Ralph. "Stephen Crane and the Mainstream of American Fiction." In *Shadow and Act,* 60–75. New York: Random House, 1964.

Franchere, Ruth. *Stephen Crane.* New York: Cromwell, 1961.

Gibson, Donald B. "'The Blue Hotel' and the Idea of Human Courage." *Texas Studies in Literature and Language* 6 (1964): 388–97.

———. *The Fiction of Stephen Crane.* Carbondale: Southern Illinois University Press, 1968.

Greenfield, Stanley B. "The Unmistakable Stephen Crane." *PMLA* 73 (1958): 562–72.

Gross, Theodore L., and Stanley Wertheim. *Hawthorne, Melville, Stephen Crane: A Critical Bibliography.* New York: Free Press, 1971.

Gullason, Thomas A., ed. *Stephen Crane's Career: Perspectives and Evaluations.* New York: New York University Press, 1972.

Hart, John E. *"The Red Badge of Courage* as Myth and Symbol." *University of Kansas City Review* 19 (1953): 249–56.

Hoffman, Daniel G. *The Poetry of Stephen Crane.* New York: Columbia University Press, 1957.

Holton, Milne. *Cylinder of Vision: The Fiction and Journalistic Writing of Stephen Crane.* Baton Rouge: Louisiana State University Press, 1972.

Johnson, George W. "Stephen Crane's Metaphor of Decorum." *PMLA* 78 (1963): 250–56.

Katz, Joseph. *The Merrill Checklist of Stephen Crane.* Columbus, Ohio: Merrill, 1969.

———, ed. *Stephen Crane in Transition: Centenary Essays.* DeKalb: Northern Illinois University Press, 1972.

Kazin, Alfred. "American Fin de Siècle." In *On Native Grounds.* New York: Reynal & Hitchcock, 1942.

LaFrance, Marston. *A Reading of Stephen Crane.* Oxford: Clarendon Press, 1971.

Lavers, Norman. "Order in *The Red Badge of Courage.*" *University of Kansas City Review* 32 (1966): 287–95.

Linson, Corwin K. *My Stephen Crane.* Syracuse, N.Y.: Syracuse University Press, 1958.

Miller, Ruth. "Regions of the Snow: The Poetic Style of Stephen Crane." *Bulletin of the New York Public Library* 72 (1968): 328–49.

Modern Fiction Studies 5 (1959). Special Stephen Crane issue.

Murphy, Brenda. "A Woman with Weapons: The Victor in Stephen Crane's *George's Mother.*" *Modern Language Studies* 11 (1981): 88–93.

Nagel, James. *Stephen Crane and Literary Impressionism.* University Park: Pennsylvania State University Press, 1980.

Neglia, Erminio G. "Fictional Death in Stephen Crane's 'The Blue Hotel' and Jorge Luis Borges 'El Sur.' " *Chasqui* 10 (1981): 20–25.

Nelson, Harlan D. "Stephen Crane's Achievement as a Poet." *Texas Studies in Literature and Language* 4 (1963): 564–82.

Pizer, Donald. "Stephen Crane's *Maggie* and American Naturalism." *Criticism* 7 (1965): 168–75.

Pritchett, V. S. "Introduction." In *The Red Badge of Courage and Other Stories.* London: World Classics, 1960.

Proudfit, Charles L. "Parataxic Distortion and Group Process in Stephen Crane's 'The Blue Hotel.' " *University of Hartford Studies in Literature* 15 (1983): 47–54.

Rahv, Philip. "Fiction and the Criticism of Fiction." *Kenyon Review* 18 (1956): 276–99.

Schneider, Robert W. "Stephen Crane: The Promethean Revolt." In *Five Novelists of the Progressive Era,* 60–111. New York: Columbia University Press, 1965.

Shatterfield, Ben. "From Romance to Reality: The Accomplishment of Private Fleming." *College Language Association Journal* 24 (1981): 451–64.

Smith, Allen Gardner. "Stephen Crane, Impressionism and William James." *Revue Français d'Etudes Américaines* 8 (1983): 237–48.

Solomon, Eric. *Stephen Crane in England.* Columbus: Ohio State University Press, 1965.

Solomon, M. "Stephen Crane: A Critical Study." *Masses and Mainstream* 9 (1956): 25–42.

Stallman, R. W. *Stephen Crane.* New York: Braziller, 1968.

———. *Stephen Crane: A Critical Bibliography.* Ames: Iowa State University Press, 1972.

Studies in the Novel 10 (1978): Special Stephen Crane issue.

Taylor, Gordon O. "The Laws of Life: Stephen Crane." In *The Passages of Thought.* New York: Oxford University Press, 1969.

Trilling, Lionel. "The Roots of Modern Taste and William Dean Howells." *Adelphi* 1 (1952): 499–516.

Tuttleton, James W. "The Imagery of *The Red Badge of Courage.*" *Modern Fiction Studies* 8 (1962): 410–15.

Weatherford, Richard M., ed. *Stephen Crane: The Critical Heritage.* London: Routledge & Kegan Paul, 1973.

Weiss, Daniel. "*The Red Badge of Courage.*" *Psychoanalytic Review* 52 (1952): 32–52, 130–54.

Westbrook, Max. "Stephen Crane's Poetry: Perspective and Arrogance." *Bucknell Review* 11 (1963): 24–34.

Wolford, Chester L. *The Anger of Stephen Crane.* Lincoln: University of Nebraska Press, 1983.

Wright, Morehead. "The Existential Adventurer and War: Three Case Studies from American Fiction." In *America Thinking about Peace and War,* 100–110. New York: Barnes & Noble, 1978.

Acknowledgments

"The Color of This Soul" by John Berryman from *Stephen Crane* by John Berryman, © 1950 by William Sloane Associates. Reprinted by permission of Meridian Publishers.

"Love on Earth" by Daniel G. Hoffman from *The Poetry of Stephen Crane* by Daniel G. Hoffman, © 1956 by Columbia University Press. Reprinted by permission.

"Stephen Crane and the Wrath of Jehova" by Stanley Wertheim from *Literary Review* 7, no. 4 (Summer 1964), © 1964 by *Literary Review*. Reprinted by permission of the author and *Literary Review*.

"'The Blue Hotel'" (originally entitled "*The Red Badge of Courage*") by Daniel Weiss from *The Critic Agonistes: Psychology, Myth and the Art of Fiction*, edited by Eric Solomon and Stephen Arkin, © 1985 by the University of Washington Press. Reprinted by permission.

"'The Open Boat'" (originally entitled "The Matter That Pleased Himself") by Marston LaFrance from *A Reading of Stephen Crane* by Marston LaFrance, © 1971 by Oxford University Press. Reprinted by permission.

"Experiments in Another Country: Stephen Crane's City Sketches" by Alan Trachtenberg from *The Southern Review* 10, no. 2 (April 1974), © 1974 by Alan Trachtenberg. Reprinted by permission.

"Stephen Crane and the Narrative Methods of Impressionism" by James Nagel from *Studies in the Novel* 10, no. 1 (Spring 1978), © 1978 by North Texas State University. Reprinted by permission.

"Vitalism and Redemptive Violence" by Harold Kaplan from *Power and Order: Henry Adams and the Naturalist Tradition in American Fiction* by Harold Kaplan, © 1981 by The University of Chicago. Reprinted by permission of The University of Chicago Press.

"Stephen Crane and the Fallen Women" by Carol Hurd Green from *American Novelists Revisited: Essays in Feminist Criticism*, edited by Fritz Fleischmann, © 1982 by Fritz Fleischmann. Reprinted by permission of the editor and Twayne Publishers, a division of G. K. Hall & Co., Boston.

161

Index

Active Service, 114; names in, 21; narrative method in, 84; Cora Stewart and, 104–6; women's role in, 20, 103

Adams, R. P., 58

Africa, symbolism of, in Crane's works, 13–15, 17. See also Blacks

"A man adrift on a slim spar," 1, 61

"A naked woman and a dead dwarf, " 101, 102–3

"Angel Child, The," 18, 112

Aretè, 135; as opposed to Christian values, 122, 123; Crane's mockery of, 140; in the epic, 118–19; of Henry Fleming, 120, 122, 129. See also Epic

Barr, Robert, 10, 26

Beer, Thomas, 9, 13, 36; on Crane's love poetry, 29; on fear in Crane's works, 7

Benjamin, Walter, 73–74

Berryman, John, 141, 143; on Crane's relations with women, 27, 29–33, 37, 100; on "The Five White Mice," 54; on Maggie, 28; on War Is Kind, 33

Binder, Henry, 137

Black, Nora (Active Service), 19–20; Cora Stewart as prototype for, 104–6

Black Riders, The: imagery in, 17, 23, 36; and "Intrigue," 29; religious conflict in, 46

Blacks, and symbolism in Crane's works, 13–15, 18–19, 32. See also Africa Blanc, Mr. See Easterner, the

Blood of the Martyr, The, 20

"Blue Hotel, The," 1, 22, 26, 131, 141; fear in, 49–54; games in, 51–52; homosexuality in, 52–54; and Ernest Hemingway's "The Killers," 49; names in, 16, 17, 18, 32; narrative method in, 88; and The Red Badge of Courage, 50, 52

Bowen, Mrs., See Watts, Doris

"Bride Comes to Yellow Sky, The," 1, 131; narrative method in, 82–83, 88; women in, 103

Brooks, Sydney, 82

Chaffee, Mrs., Stephen Crane and, 12

Christian collective ideal. See Pietas

"City sketches," 65–79

Civil War, the, 1, 4, 97; Crane's interest in, 14, 32, 91. See also The Red Badge of Courage; "Three Miraculous Soldiers"; Warfare

"Clan of No Name, The, " 10, 15, 21

Clark, Dora, Stephen Crane and, 9, 28, 31, 110

Clarke, Willis, 13

Claverack, 12, 17, 115

Coleman, Rufus (Active Service), 103–4, 106

Conklin, Jim (The Red Badge of Courage), 26, 123; character of, 47; as Christ figure, 120, 121–22, 124, 126–27; death of, 92–93, 109; name of, 24; and Wilson, 128

Conrad, Joseph, 1, 2

Crane, Cora Howarth Taylor Stewart. See Stewart, Cora

Crane, Helen Peck, 13; Crane's relationship with, 9, 11, 23–24, 112; religious beliefs of, 41–42; as rescuer, 9, 111

Crane, Jonathan Townley: Stephen Crane's rebellion against, 43–44, 45–46; Stephen Crane's relationship with, 11, 12, 15; and influence on Stephen Crane, 107, 109–10; religious beliefs of, 41, 42–43, 44. Works: Arts of Intoxication, 42; An Essay on Dancing, 42; Holiness, the Birthright of All God's Children, 42, 107; Popular Amusements, 42; The Right Way, 42

Modern Critical Views

Continued from front of book

Gabriel García Márquez
Andrew Marvell
Carson McCullers
Herman Melville
George Meredith
James Merrill
John Stuart Mill
Arthur Miller
Henry Miller
John Milton
Yukio Mishima
Molière
Michel de Montaigne
Eugenio Montale
Marianne Moore
Alberto Moravia
Toni Morrison
Alice Munro
Iris Murdoch
Robert Musil
Vladimir Nabokov
V. S. Naipaul
R. K. Narayan
Pablo Neruda
John Henry, Cardinal
    Newman
Friedrich Nietzsche
Frank Norris
Joyce Carol Oates
Sean O'Casey
Flannery O'Connor
Christopher Okigbo
Charles Olson
Eugene O'Neill
José Ortega y Gasset
Joe Orton
George Orwell
Ovid
Wilfred Owen
Amos Oz
Cynthia Ozick
Grace Paley
Blaise Pascal
Walter Pater
Octavio Paz
Walker Percy
Petrarch
Pindar
Harold Pinter
Luigi Pirandello
Sylvia Plath
Plato

Plautus
Edgar Allan Poe
Poets of Sensibility & the
    Sublime
Poets of the Nineties
Alexander Pope
Katherine Anne Porter
Ezra Pound
Anthony Powell
Pre-Raphaelite Poets
Marcel Proust
Manuel Puig
Alexander Pushkin
Thomas Pynchon
Francisco de Quevedo
François Rabelais
Jean Racine
Ishmael Reed
Adrienne Rich
Samuel Richardson
Mordecai Richler
Rainer Maria Rilke
Arthur Rimbaud
Edwin Arlington Robinson
Theodore Roethke
Philip Roth
Jean-Jacques Rousseau
John Ruskin
J. D. Salinger
Jean-Paul Sartre
Gershom Scholem
Sir Walter Scott
William Shakespeare
    (3 vols.)
    Histories & Poems
    Comedies & Romances
    Tragedies
George Bernard Shaw
Mary Wollstonecraft
    Shelley
Percy Bysshe Shelley
Sam Shepard
Richard Brinsley Sheridan
Sir Philip Sidney
Isaac Bashevis Singer
Tobias Smollett
Alexander Solzhenitsyn
Sophocles
Wole Soyinka
Edmund Spenser
Gertrude Stein
John Steinbeck

Stendhal
Laurence Sterne
Wallace Stevens
Robert Louis Stevenson
Tom Stoppard
August Strindberg
Jonathan Swift
John Millington Synge
Alfred, Lord Tennyson
William Makepeace
    Thackeray
Dylan Thomas
Henry David Thoreau
James Thurber and S. J.
    Perelman
J. R. R. Tolkien
Leo Tolstoy
Jean Toomer
Lionel Trilling
Anthony Trollope
Ivan Turgenev
Mark Twain
Miguel de Unamuno
John Updike
Paul Valéry
Cesar Vallejo
Lope de Vega
Gore Vidal
Virgil
Voltaire
Kurt Vonnegut
Derek Walcott
Alice Walker
Robert Penn Warren
Evelyn Waugh
H. G. Wells
Eudora Welty
Nathanael West
Edith Wharton
Patrick White
Walt Whitman
Oscar Wilde
Tennessee Williams
William Carlos Williams
Thomas Wolfe
Virginia Woolf
William Wordsworth
Jay Wright
Richard Wright
William Butler Yeats
A. B. Yehoshua
Emile Zola